LIVING IN OUR FINEST HOUR

A Journey Beyond Salvation

DOUGLAS COOPER

Pacific Press Publishing Association
Mountain View, California
Oshawa, Ontario

Second Printing, 1983

Cover photo by Ed Cooper

Copyright © 1982 by
Pacific Press Publishing Association
Printed in United States of America
All Rights Reserved

Library of Congress Cataloging in Publication Data

Cooper, Douglas.
  Living in our finest hour.

  (Redwood)
  Includes bibliographical references.
    1. Christian life—1960-   2. Baptism in the Holy Spirit.
I. Title.
BV4501.2.C6773   248.4'8673   81-22318
ISBN 0-8163-0465-3   AACR2

ISBN 0-8163-0465-3

Contents

1

Our Finest Hour

For, behold, the darkness shall cover the earth,
and gross darkness the people:
but the Lord shall arise upon thee,
and his glory shall be seen upon thee.

Isaiah 60:2.

In the darkest hour in the history of the modern world the monstrous tyranny of Nazi domination held the forces of decency and justice at bay. Foreboding filled the hearts of all free men. Great Britain, the nation which had cradled democracy in its infancy, was being deliberately, tortuously ground to destruction under the heel of pitiless oppressor.

It was as if the legions of evil had conspired in wicked revenge to punish this land for daring to give freedom its wings, for daring to have served as the launching pad of Christianity to the New World.

At this hour one man stepped to the center stage of history. A man under the direction of God. His words were heard clearly across the length and breadth of the besieged nation. They have come to be immortalized.

"I have nothing to offer but blood, toil, tears and sweat. We have before us an ordeal of the most grievous kind. We have before us many very long months of struggling and suffering. . . . Come then, let us go forward together with our united strength."

Nevertheless, calamity followed on calamity. The

United Kingdom's allies were being picked off one by one. Belgium fell, leaving the British soldiers on the Continent to face the huge armies of the enemy alone. At Dunkirk, in retreat, with nowhere else to go, a British army of more than a third of a million men was being pushed into the sea on the French side of the English Channel. All of their equipment lost, thirty thousand men were killed or captured.

The cowardly Mussolini chose this opportune time to declare war on Britain. Shortly thereafter France surrendered. Would Britain too be overwhelmed as well?

The world trembled as it began to realize what the outcome of this momentous struggle might mean. The tiny island country had become the last stronghold in all Europe for truth and freedom. Winston Churchill expressed it exquisitely: "If we fail, then the whole world . . . will sink into the abyss of a new Dark Age, made more sinister and perhaps more protracted by the lights of perverted science."

The British people began to prepare for the worst. It seemed a certainty that the enemy would soon touch their beaches, land in their fields, march in their streets. In unforgettable words, Churchill hurled the challenge: "We shall defend our island whatever the cost may be. We shall fight on the beaches, we shall fight on the landing grounds, we shall fight in the fields and in the streets. We shall fight in the hills; We shall never surrender. . . .

"The battle of France is over. I expect that the battle of Britain is about to begin. Upon that battle depends the survival of Christian civilization."

Next he uttered the magnificent words that symbolize the meaning of this book. "Let us therefore, brace ourselves to our duties and so bear ourselves that, if the British Empire and its Commonwealth last for a thousand years, men will say, 'This was their finest hour.' "[1]

A similar conflict today rages in the world, one which far exceeds in its magnitude and consequence that faced by the British people. The battle of this hour is waged not for occupation of land or control of sea. It is waged singularly for the very souls of human beings. The destiny, not of one nation, not even of one civilization, but of all mankind hangs in the balance. Strange struggle—a person in the midst of it may be totally unaware of it. It is indeed the ultimate contest of the ages in which only the alert, the discerning, will be victorious.

Squarely at the forefront, love is pitted against selfishness, two forces which are absolute antithesis. When each is in its purest form, when each is personified, as it is in the case of Christ and Satan, they cannot abide in the company of one another. Integration of the two is impossible. Selfishness and love can never be synthesized successfully in any life, in any nation, on any planet.

Since that unprecedented event, the entrance of selfishness—or, as some call it, sin—into the universe, the world has reeled under the impact of these two factors confronting each other. Now, on this planet there is disharmony, conflict, and eruptive confusion. Lawlessness grapples with lawfulness. Unholiness struggles with holiness. Death attempts to choke out life, as evil wills to destroy all that is good.

Two mighty powers here meet. One alone will conquer!

At His cross Jesus Christ exposed Satan to the universe as the true enemy of all good. With his wicked motives and the extent of his degeneracy now flushed into the open, Satan no longer hides his desperation. His original desire to conquer and destroy all that is

7

good and godlike he has fanned to a fiendish passion. Consumed with a furious fervor to annihilate the kingdom of love, he comes brazenly to the hour of his final stand. Using every weapon in his unsavory arsenal, he is making a frenzied play to attempt to keep control of hijacked *Spaceship Earth* and its human passengers. Although because of the cross he cannot now use his victims to force his will against the government of the universe, his insane selfishness still compels him to drag as many of his hostages as he can over the brink to eternal ruin with him. These efforts have succeeded in bringing the world to this crisis hour.

Another startling victory is his success in blinding of so many to what is happening. This plot-master dulls human awareness to the point where most can no longer discern the issues, no longer discriminate between evil and good, selfishness and love, right and wrong. He clouds the issues, destroys the absolutes, and removes the pillars. Human beings, children of God, left confused in a gray haze, have become accustomed to selfishness and evil that they accept them as normal.

One indication of Satan's success is the world's murderously insane arms race. Only a fiend could have generated the sort of atmosphere in the world today that seduces each of the major governments of the world to attempt to top the other in the number of times it can destroy the other. Satan has so locked the world into this spinning self-destructive cycle that the keenest of minds can find no way to break free.

Another indication of his success is widespread depravity. Seldom have morality and decency reached such low points. Chastity? It is a laughingstock. Virtue? A novelty. Violence and illicit sex have become the chief form of entertainment and for some are the chief form of recreation! Satan has found a master strategy: Destroy the best citadel in the world of true love—the faithful marriage relationship—and everything else will fall with it.

Unique too, in all the history of the world, is the abuse of technology. A handful of ruthless men can threaten the peace and security of the strongest, most civilized nations on earth with heretofore unheard of terrorist acts of kidnapping, sabotage, and assassination. Evil is brasher, bolder, more totally destructive and uncaring than ever before.

Even the economic security of the world is held together by nothing more than a very fragile thread. With nowhere to turn for true financial security, men's hearts are 'failing them for fear.''[2] In times past, when problems arose, when difficulties needed to be surmounted, there was always promise of an answer being provided by new ideas, new technology, new leadership. Only in the last few years have governments had to face the stark reality that truly *unsolvable* problems now confront them. The "ultimate panacea for all humanity's ills"—modern science—has proven totally inadequate. *The human intellect in all disciplines, even when stretched to its limit, now appears incapable of solving the difficulties of the human heart and soul.* As never before, events of today cry out in one great voice that the climax of the ages is at hand!

Too often Christians have focused on sin's latest triumphs as proof that something exceptional is soon to occur. Ask yourself this question: *As evil grows continually more aggressive, can we expect a corresponding surge of good?* As liars abound, can we foresee an increase in the number who value truth above all else? As fornicators multiply, can we anticipate a proliferation of the pure? As evil's champions gain ever greater and ever more eager followings, can we look forward to seeing new heroes of God arise? As Goliaths boastfully strut the plain, do we have in prospect any Davids?

The challenge of this hour appears to be this: The increasing intensity of evil and selfishness in some *must be matched* by a parallel increase of love and righteousness in others. When iniquity abounds, grace and goodness must much more abound.

But this cannot happen unless with a special perspective people see evil for what it really is and good for what it is. People must be willing to invest "blood, toil, tears, and sweat" and to stand against the forces of selfishness and ungodliness. People must recognize the special chance that is theirs to align with God's cause of righteousness and love and must be willing to defend their faith in God to the death if necessary.

In the hour of greatest darkness, more brightly burns the candle. The Bible says, "The spirit of man is the candle of the Lord."[3] Those of us who live today, as the darkest hours of earth's history approach, have the unique opportunity to contribute more to the victorious climax of God's campaign to eliminate sin and selfishness from the universe than any other generation since the world began.

There is no more exciting hour to be alive. *There have never been, nor will there ever be, greater challenges or more magnificent opportunities to accomplish, to contribute, and to serve.* The stakes have never been higher, but neither have the rewards and satisfactions ever been greater.

As evil's attacks become keener, the resources and countermeasures available to those who would stand for truth become more abundant. After all, we live on the "victory side" of the cross! We benefit immensely from the effect that two thousand years of this antidote for sin has had. The witness of Jesus Christ's life, death, resurrection, and intercession; the ministry of angels; the mighty indwelling presence, power, and gifts of the Holy Spirit; the work of God the Father above and through all; the unceasing concern of heavenly beings; and the eager willingness of divinity to couple with humanity, all combine to place at the Christian's disposal an unconquerable arsenal against evil!

Yet, where are the people—God's heroes—who will step into the battle and use these marvelous spiritual tools for God? Our heavenly Father has chosen to make Himself dependent *on people* to finish His conquest of sin. It will be the cooperation of human beings with divine beings that will defeat evil permanently. In a strange and ironic turnabout Satan is to be "bested" by the members of the very race he led astray! Nothing could demonstrate more effectively the superiority of love over selfishness, the power of compassion over coercion!

His honor, His very name and reputation in the universe rest in your hands and mine. *For this reason Christians are the most important people in the world right now!*

"Be not overcome of evil, but overcome evil with good."[4] At this crucial hour will you be seduced by the subtle allure of evil? Or will you choose to be among those who contribute in the divine conquering?

The final dramatic conflict between the forces of good and evil will be resolved not on some far-off galactic battlefield. Satan will be permanently defeated in the life of each individual human being who chooses to live completely for love, for God who is love.

Your life, your personality, your character stands center stage. Yours is the last act in the great drama of the ages.

God needs people. People who insist on showing themselves stubbornly true to principle. People who,

11

when the religion of Christ is held in coldest contempt, will show their zeal to be the warmest. People who, when His law is most despised, will reveal their courage and firmness to be the most unflinching. People who, when the world majority has forsaken such qualities as unessential, will stand as flesh-and-blood examples of unselfish love and uncompromising truth.

At the close of the conflict a group of individuals will see the honor of God vindicated before the universe in their own lives. They will have demonstrated the depths of His unconditional love. They will actually have established such oneness with Him that His thoughts will have become their thoughts; His ways, their ways; His character, theirs. They will have resisted evil at the peak of its fury. They will have allowed God to defeat it once and for all on the very turf of their own lives. Certainly not by their own wisdom or personal piety or persistence. *Victory will be theirs because of the closeness they sought and the dependence they have chosen on the Christ who indwells them so completely by the Holy Spirit.*

Soon the controversy will end. The entire universe will once again exist in peace and harmony. One pulse of love will beat in unison throughout all God's vast creation.

As for those who were given the privilege of helping to make this splendid situation a reality—perhaps they can look back from the vantage point of eternity to that time when they stood loyally for God to defeat evil and say, "That was our finest hour!"

2

Where the Action Is

Jesus Said . . . , Follow me.
Matthew 8:22.

I wish I could have known the uncle I was named after. They tell me he was very good-looking, over six feet tall, with dark, wavy hair. Leafing through the old family album when I was a child, I remember always pausing whenever I came to his picture. He looked so handsome in his uniform. His soft smile seemed genuine. There was determination in the set of his eyes.

It must have grown to be a burning compulsion to my uncle, that urge to get involved, to do his part. Strong, eager, concerned, he could not sit by merely as a spectator. Seeing rising evil power threatening the things he believed in and the people he loved, he determined to fight it.

Since Canada had immediate openings for flight training in its armed forces, he went north to enlist. Pilot officer Douglas Dean won his Royal Canadian Air Force pilot's wings—and at the controls of a Royal Canadian Air Force plane he died.

I still have his faded now, photograph, his war medals, and the letter of condolence from the king of England. I have already given the medals to my own son, who also carries my uncle's name.

Many today need to open their eyes to the truly momentous moral and spiritual issues at stake. If they could gain insight into the play and counterplay occuring between the unseen forces of good and evil, the mounting tension between morality and immorality, the extensive mingling of truth with error, they would become so alarmed and concerned they—like my uncle—would instantly be shaken into action.

In the present struggle no one can hope to maintain indifference or neutrality. Not to decide is to decide. To attempt to remain unconcerned and uninvolved is to lend support to the forces of darkness. As Edmund Burke said, "All that is necessary for evil to triumph is for good men to do nothing."

How unfortunate that as the climax hour of earth's history approaches, so many are now unseeing, uncaring, unwilling to become involved in the great issues. Do we have today a generation of spectators on this planet? Never before have so many been so little involved with anything but their own interests and pleasures. *Never before have the lives of so many consisted of what they see and hear—instead of what they do and are.*

There are spectator sports, spectator politics, spectator entertainment, and spectator religion. Many delude themselves into thinking that by observing they are part of something interesting and exciting and productive while actually they *do* and *accomplish* nothing. The vicarious excitement of spectating immunizes with enough artificial stimuli to keep one from thinking too deeply. It prevents people from becoming involved in *real* action, from taking *real* risks, and from having *real* accomplishments. Spectatorism, rampant today, is dangerous because it diminishes reality for those caught up in it as it diminishes their individuality and creativity.

The few are so involved in meaningful, constructive *action*, while the many are frustrated. Some are involved physically, but very few morally and spiritually. Yet in these twin arenas of the human soul people *really live*. Here the great battles of the day rage. If you are going to make a contribution in your lifetime, you must refuse to let yourself be caught up in the popular, spectator mentality of these times. You must also have something more to live for than acquiring possessions. There are goals with more meaning than early retirement and settling back in to a life of comfortable ease.

The myopia of modern materialism prevents people today from understanding and becoming constructively involved with the needs and issues of the hour. "A man's life," Jesus warned, "consisteth not in the abundance of the things which he possesseth."[1]

Anyone who equates success and happiness with the collection of material things misses the point of life. The struggle to acquire more and more possesions renders one incapable of gaining the insight or making the commitment necessary to contribute to the final victory of love over selfishness, of good over evil.

Jesus Christ came claiming He had come to deliver men from evil and to set people free. "Seek ye first the kingdom of God," He said; "Labour not for the meat which perisheth"; and "Lay not up for yourselves treasures on earth."[2] Centuries later the modern psychologist William James wrote, "Lives based on having are less free than lives based on doing or being."

Clearly, those who wholeheartedly enlist on the side of right against selfishness and evil will be those unusual individuals who willingly give their best, *not to get more, but to be more and do more*.

You may have heard of the three great classes into which society tends to divide. True of secular society, the observations are also true of the spiritual and moral realm. These are, *number one,* people who make things happen; *number two,* people who watch and talk about things that are happening (the spectators); and, *number three,* people who do not even know what is happening. Into which category do you fit? If you truly wish to be in the first group, you will align yourself as closely as possible with Jesus Christ and His concepts of ministering and unconditional love. He is where the real action is today. It is not possible to follow Him without involvement and commitment to the vital issues in the world today. To sidestep these and center your life around something else is to deny Him. "The most prominent place in hell," Billy Graham has said, "is reserved for those who are neutral on the great issues of life."

According to the Bible, those who do nothing—though they may have lived good, moral, orderly lives—will be found wanting before the judgment bar of God just as surely as those who deliberately disobey.

George Small has written the following:

I read in a book
where a man called Jesus Christ
went about doing good.
Why is it that I am so easily satisfied
with just going about?

Christ was indeed a totally dynamic Person, a Man of action. He knew that the great end of life was not material possessions or knowledge, but meaningful action. Christianity consists of *action.* Christianity encourages, even compels men to be more than spectators. It gives the clearest vision that men can have into the meaning of life, a vision which reveals that living indeed amounts to more than what you see, what you

16

hear, and what you manage to acquire or control.

Through the centuries Christianity has never failed to inspire men to great acts of service, great acts of faith. It has prompted them to growth, to productivity, to creativity, even to genius. It has shown complacency to be an unaffordable element of life.

Four thousand years of proliferating evil had dragged the entire human race into a physical and spiritual abyss when Jesus came. No one had been able to checkmate evil until then. Men's best intentions and attempts had proven fruitless. In vain were their dreams of progress, in vain their efforts for uplifting humanity. But Jesus came, and with Him the hope for a new tomorrow. He alone possessed the power to conquer evil. His love was big enough to defeat selfishness. His perfect life, His atoning death turned the tide.

The cross brought Satan and his forces to the beginning of their end and decided the final conquest of sin. Evil has been on the defensive ever since. Men began to sense the power of Christianity. It was the power to live, the power to do what could not be done before. It spread like a wonderful contagion. It toppled the materialistic, idol-worshiping Roman Empire. It swept on—changing, stimulating, enlightening. It gave birth to concepts of modern democratic civilization. It ignited the explosion of knowledge that began to free men from tyranny and poverty and disease. In a profound sense the teachings of Jesus Christ have moved mankind out of the dark age into the space age! Think about it. Is it any coincidence that the nations that are or have been the most Christian are also the most progressive and most advanced of all in the areas of freedom, human rights, living standards, and equal opportunities for everyone?

The United States, founded on Christian principles, rose in a remarkably short time to lead the world. It still has the resources and compassion to reach out to other nations in time of need and calamity. It has become a caring big brother to the entire world. Its technology has been so successfully advanced that it is now responsible for 28 percent of the world's product, yet contains only 5 percent of the population! When American farmers finish feeding their own countrymen, they still have nearly 50 percent of all their major crops left to export to others that need them. When an earthquake or flood strikes some other country America is usually first on the scene to help and to heal. Other countries of the world have a similar capacity to provide for other's needs and a similiar inclination to do it, but interestingly enough they too are the countries of the world who are founded on Christian principles of freedom and concern for the individual. Jesus predicted long ago that those who would be guided in their actions by His Spirit of unselfish love would have from them flowing "rivers of living waters" to support and nourish others.[3]

The intellectual and social climate caused by the impact of Christ's teachings on the world produced the sort of atmosphere in which America could rise and prosper.

Wherever it has gone, Christianity has inspired, uplifted, and stimulated to dynamic action. It has made producers and not just consumers, doers and not just hearers. It has enlivened people intellectually and morally. It has brought them face-to-face with new goals, new challenges, new ideals. It insistently reminds them that real life consists not of living for self, but for others.

If Jesus Christ had not stepped onto the stage of earth's history, I would go so far as to say, the entire human race, spurred on by the evil genius of Satan, would by now have sunk into such an abyss of selfishness and degeneracy it would have self-destructed. Only the impact Christianity has on individual lives, I believe, has prevented this from happening. *It is the change within the human heart, the amazing restructuring of the character and personality, the redefinition of motives and goals, the reordering of priorities and emotions that makes the religion of Jesus such a vital force.*

Christ changes lives. He makes the drunkard sober, the profligate pure, the selfish loving. By choosing to allow Him to do it, you may experience Christ beginning to move you away from the life of selfishness, defeat, and unproductivity, and to guide you toward the highest and best kind of fulfillment.

Jesus Christ alone can truly make a man all he was meant to be. No life is centered in reality until it is centered in Him, who said, "I am the way the truth, and the life."[4] Was He a liar, the greatest liar and imposter who has ever duped the world? Or was He who He said He was—the Son of God?

Through the splendid vision Christ alone gives, a person discovers the value and meaning of his life. He can define success for himself. He can discern what is worth living for and what worth dying for. No longer merely existing, he is freed to become really *alive*. "As life is action and passion," Oliver Wendell Holmes, Jr. wrote, "it is required of man that he should share the passion and action of his time, at peril of being judged not to have lived."

So if you wish to be where the real action is . . . if you want your life to count for some great good . . . if you want to be a doer and not just a spectator . . . if you are so offended by death and despair and pain and suffering that you wish to contribute to Christ's final conquest . . . then center your life around Him.

Jesus is either too good to be true, or so good He must be true. You must either accept or reject Him. He cannot be ignored. "He that is not with me," He said, "is against me."[5]

This choice need not be complicated or traumatic. He does not demand some spectacular mental struggle. There is nothing to change or give up before He will accept you. You need only to respond to His invitation to something better than and beyond the natural human life. Accept Him as the terminally ill patient accepts the physician who can cure him. It can be as easy as saying, "I do," to your bride or groom. You need only to say, "I will," to Him who gently asks, "Follow me".

"And Jesus, walking by the sea of Galilee, saw two brethren, Simon called Peter and Andrew his brother, casting a net into the sea: for they were fishers. And He said unto them, Follow me, and I will make you fishers of men."[6]

Picture this: Two simple fishermen, uneducated, unrefined, ply their trade as did their fathers before them. Their entire existence centers around the day-to-day struggle to earn a living. Fishing is all they knew, their whole life. They have freedom to hesitate, to wait for more facts to come in or for some great urgency. But somehow they sense that failing to decide would be equivalent to saying no.

Scripture tells us their response: "They straightway left their nets, and followed him."[7]

The two fishermen accepted a simple, straightforward invitation. *And their lives were never the same again*. They stepped onto history's center stage. Caught up in some of the most profound events of all time, they wrestled with concepts and truths of eternal magnitude. Drawn into the thick of the action, they received unlimited opportunities to learn, to grow and to contribute. By choosing Jesus, they found the opportunity of a lifetime. This same Jesus offers the same chance to you—right now.

Christ gave the same invitation to another, a man of great wealth, power, position and education. Jesus looked through all this, straight into his heart. There He saw the young man's deep dependence on the "things" he possessed in abundance. With supernatural acuity He tested him on one issue: "Go and sell (what) thou hast, and give to the poor, and thou shalt have treasure in heaven: and come and follow me. But when the young man heard that saying, he went away sorrowful: for he had great possessions."[8] From this point on the young man is lost to history. Imagine what he could have become!

Many have speculated. Would he have written a fifth gospel? "The Gospel According to the (Formerly) Rich Young Man." His name might have been among the all-time heroes of the Christian faith—those who "turned the world upside down." He may never have seen his earthly riches restored—or, again, he may—but one thing is certain: *He would have received eternal life*.

Today the call to the fishermen of Galilee is still heard. Your response can assure you both "treasure in heaven" and a place in the action in earth's last great crises.

3

Beyond Salvation

How to Be All That You Can Be

*We ought not to be laying over again
the foundations of faith in God and of
repentance. . . . Instead, let us advance
towards maturity. Hebrews 6:1-3, NEB.*

Walking home from school, I came across them occasionally. Strange tracks in the snow. Had an animal been dragging something away?

My parents and I lived beside a large lake in western Alaska. In the winter I often followed the dog-team trail from my home to the little village schoolhouse or when I returned at the end of the day on the snow-covered ice. For a while I was very puzzled over the tracks. Then one day I realized they belonged to Antone, "the man who walks like a bear."

The other Eskimos called him that. And from a distance that was certainly what he resembled. Crawling over the snow in his squirrel-skin parka and beaver hat, he did look more animal than human. His small, wizened body was distorted by a disease. His spine twisted, hunchbacked and partially paralyzed from the waist down, he would never straighten or stand.

It seems he would have quickly resigned himself to the confines of an invalid's bed, but not Antone. At some time in his life he had decided what he was going to do and be. In the Alaskan "bush" village of thirty years ago there were no wheelchairs or even cars or buses. If Antone wanted to go somewhere, he half-dragged his nearly useless legs behind him. In the cold snow, using his powerful arms and shoulders, he propelled himself forward. Or, if going far, he would harness his dog team and drive it. He rode the runners on his knees, clinging tightly to the handlebars. He would go into the forest to cut wood to keep his log cabin warm for his wife and three daughters. Quite a job? Have you ever tried chopping wood while kneeling in three feet of snow? He also had to wrestle the logs onto the sled, drive them back to his cabin and unload them.

Like other Eskimo families of that time, his family depended largely on the food the father hunted. Antone excelled at being a good provider. He could shoot and butcher a thousand-pound moose as quickly as any other. Many times I saw him hunting ducks and geese on the lake with his kayak. He was better than anyone else in the village at paddling the little skin boat around because of his powerfully developed upper body and because he was so adept at kneeling. He would bring ducks in and give them to the other men of the village who were not so adept. In the summer he used a small outboard-powered boat to work his salmon nets. Once I watched him single-handedly wrestle a three-hundred-pound barrel of gasoline out of this boat. He rolled it uphill on the beach to a storage area, pushing on it with his mighty back and shoulders and dragging his legs along behind him.

To my knowledge Antone never asked for, expected, or received any extra help from any of the other men of the village. At that time this seemed cruel to me. At this time, though, I am sure that he would never have accepted any.

His cabin was not far from our home. Sometimes we would hear the heavy thump of a mittened fist on our door. Like any eager youngster I would run to open it. Glancing upward as usual, I would see no one. Then I would look down—and see Antone crouched in the snow at my feet, looking up at me with his great grin, immensely enjoying the surprised look on my face.

Upon being invited in he would crawl into the house and position himself on the kitchen floor. He spoke English well, an uncommon knack for an Eskimo of his age at that time. He possessed a quick and active mind. My father and he would talk for hours during the long winter evenings, but I never remember him once complaining or even discussing his condition.

Youngsters sometimes make fun among themselves of someone who is different or handicapped. Even in private we village children *never* dared to mock crippled Antone. We never wanted to. We held him in awe and respect.

Even today, when I walk through a fresh snowfall, I sometimes catch myself unconsciously glancing around, looking for those strange tracks. Though there is no Antone to make them anymore, their memory always reminds me of a man who would let nothing stop him, a man who lived far beyond what anyone would expect of him, a man who lived up to *all* he possibly could be in the physical world.

In the spiritual world those who will stand for God at the climax of earth's history will be a group extraordinarily like Jesus Christ. They will be experts at loving. They will be full of unquenchable joy. They will live lives of continual victory. Though their human natures are marred by sin, they will live out their fullest spiritual potential just as my crippled Eskimo friend lived out his fullest physical potential.

No mere spectators these! Instead of exclaiming and

lamenting over evil, they will be active doing good. They will counteract evil, not merely by condemning it, but by loving and unselfish service. In the darkest hour, more brightly shines the candle. Amid the darkening shadows of earth's last night, they will reflect the saving light of God's love more splendidly than has any group of God's people since Creation.

Because man chose to separate himself from God, selfishness has replaced love as the ruling principle of the world. But Christ's death on the cross has conquered sin. *This sacrifice made the provision for the Holy Spirit to live in men a reality. Selfishness can thus be eliminated.* Love, the principle of life, regains the throne. The process begins in the lives of Christians right now. It will climax in the total annihilation of sin and establishment of a sinless new earth.

God is moving men toward the full restoration of the supremacy of love at this moment. *The ability to love perfectly will enable the character of God to so animate people today that they will provide Him with a foundation for His kingdom in this world tomorrow.* His character so infuses them that the atmosphere of heaven eventually becomes more natural to them than the atmosphere of this world. He wants them to be living as Jesus lived, not as people naturally do. Right now.

Enoch became so close and intimate with divinity, so much like his heavenly Father, that "God took him."[1] His example shows that God seeks to "naturalize" men and women into His kingdom of heaven. The spiritual development God's people will finally achieve will be gained not artificially by their own struggles to be good, but *naturally by the closeness of their walk with God*. They concentrate on this closeness to achieve success. For centuries men have tried "self-improvement" courses in a multitude of

25

ways, but always have ended up failing miserably. The problem with all human approaches is that the central figure is self. Concentration on closeness to Christ, however, centers the quest around God Himself. The secret is in abiding.

Christ has been waiting for almost two millenniums now for enough people to stop doing it their way, to stop centering their spiritual life around self. He wants them to start concentrating on closeness to Him. As Christians we approach our finest hour as Christ becomes the center of reality in more and more lives. God wants to integrate much more of the kingdom of heaven into the lives of Christians at this moment than we can possibly imagine.

The truth of salvation by faith has become so repeatedly emphasized that many have come to assume that accepting it is all there is to Christianity. *While the importance of this most magnificent doctrine of all can never be disputed, the repeated emphasis on it to the almost total exclusion of anything else has left many sincere Christians stunted and immature in their spiritual growth and strength.*

As you read these lines, you are more than likely comfortably seated in a building protected by walls and roof. Would you be so comfortable and secure if your home consisted only of a foundation but had no walls or roof? While salvation by faith is the great foundation upon which Christianity stands, it must never be considered the total structure. Righteousness by faith begins a learning process that goes on throughout eternity.

Paul laments a condition among Christians that points to what may still be the greatest weakness in the church today: "For indeed though by this time you ought to be teachers, you need someone to teach you the ABC of God's oracles over again; it has come to this, that you need milk instead of solid food. Anyone who lives on milk, being an infant, does not know what is right. But grown men can take solid food; their perceptions are trained by long use to discriminate between good and evil."[2]

After pointing out that these people are failing to be all they could be for God, the apostle goes on to make what many might consider to be a very shocking statement: *"Let us then stop discussing the rudiments of Christianity. We ought not to be laying over again the foundations of faith in God and of repentance from the deadness of our former ways. . . Instead, let us advance towards maturity."*[3]

The time comes in the Christian life, Paul says, when one must gain a correct understanding of the experience of conversion and forgiveness of sin so that he may progress on to truths more suited to maturity. What would have happened if the disciples had gotten caught up in anxious attempts continually to re-lay "the foundations of faith"? Would Pentecost ever have come? Is there nothing more in the Christian life than to keep reaffirming constantly the conversion experience of the past? Was it such an inconclusive experience?

One reason I have always enjoyed learning was Mrs. Snyder, my first-grade teacher. Her little one-room country school with its pot-bellied stove, its path to "the facilities" out back, and its "board of education" on the wall started me out on the road to literacy. A matronly figure who wore round, gold-rimmed spectacles, she treasured a heart full of kids. She made my learning an adventure. Mrs. Snyder taught me my ABCs, a skill which aided me in my understanding of such profound concepts as Dick and Jane's relationship with their canine companion Spot. How my six-year-old mind thrived! Educationally, the "Dick and

Jane level" was my level. Yet all the while, blissfully unknown to me, Mrs. Snyder cunningly was laying a valuable foundation for me. Now would I wish to go back and insult Mrs. Snyder's efforts by wedging myself in that little desk with its quaint inkwell, and working long hours copying my ABCs? *If not, then why be content to stay in spiritual kindergarten all of our spiritual lives?* Are spiritual dwarfs all we have to witness to a world in need of spiritual giants?

The preoccupation of so many with the rudiments of Christianity, salvation and justification, keep them from fulfilling God's great purpose in their lives.

God offers definite assurance of eternal life, a clearly and freely offered gift. To deny its availability now nullifies in your own life the very death of Jesus Christ on the cross, prevents God from giving you eternal life and working out His will and destiny for you, and frustrates His plan to lead you, guide you, and protect you as He would wish. For without your trust in His ultimate promise, His ultimate gift, He has no foundation in your life to build on.

Jesus said plainly, "In very truth, anyone who gives heed to what I say and puts his trust in him who sent me has hold of eternal life, and does not come up for judgment, but has already passed from death to life."[4] Preoccupation with the condemnation of sin or fear of coming up short at some future time is inappropriate and spiritually destructive for the Christian, who should rest securely on the foundation of Christ's sacrifice for him. But resting on the foundation frees the Christian to be built splendidly and extraordinarily for God. Such faith opens the way for the Holy Spirit to fill the life and begin shaping a person in the very image of Christ. It allows God to get on with His work in the life, *which is the reason for saving people in the first place.* God does not just justify a man, and then do nothing further for him. *He justifies him in order to begin re-storing in him His own image, in order to infuse him with the divine nature, the divine Spirit, the divine love, right now.* Paul refers to our Lord Jesus Christ "as the One by whom we have *now* received the atonement."[5]

Receiving salvation is not a process which takes your whole lifetime. It is the experience of a moment. The miracle gift of God becomes yours the instant you choose to accept it and it remains yours as long as you keep close to your Saviour daily. Concentrate on the closeness and let God concentrate on the righteousness. He is better at that than you are.

If you are an insecure Christian who feels, "I am working on getting ready to be saved" or "I hope that when Christ comes I will receive salvation," then you are not yet out of spiritual first grade. You limit God. He will not be able to make you all you can be for Him unless you are settled in your own mind about your own salvation.

If you stand up in church and sing "Redeemed! How I Love to Proclaim It!" but later stand up in testimony meeting and say, "Well, remember me in your prayers, friends, because I'm hoping to be saved someday," you need to accept Jesus Christ into your life right now!

The great sin committed in the Garden of Eden by our first parents was not abusing appetite, but distrusting God's goodness and disbelieving His word. You can commit that same sin just as easily today by failing to take Him at His word when He offers you salvation right now.

There should be no doubt, no confusion, no uncertainty in your mind at any given time whether or not you are saved or unsaved. If you are not saved, you can choose to be. Your status will be changed at once.

God says so. If you have already chosen Him, then rejoice and enjoy your salvation. Go on then from this firm spiritual foundation to the other great things God has in store for you. Your finest hour lies yet ahead. As God offers it, justification by faith frees you from any burden about your salvation. Once you receive it, you are at liberty instead to concentrate on your highest calling—to become full of unselfish love like Jesus Christ. You want to do this, to become this, not in order to qualify for being saved, because you already are. You do it because it is the way to total living, total wholeness. It is what you were made for. When you accept salvation, you are freed to become all you were truly meant to be.

Once you are ready for this next exciting dimension of Christianity, the dimension *beyond salvation* (in the sense "beyond pardon"), you will realize how important is the fact that the world, yes even the universe, is awaiting a convincing demonstration that Christianity really produces *better people*—not just sinners who claim eternal life.

Those who get the most out of life on earth are those who will get the most out of life in heaven. These are overcomers in the present tense. "To him that overcometh will I give to eat of the tree of life, which is in the midst of the paradise of God."[6]

Just as there is more to the Holy City than just the gateway, so there is more to Christianity than just the gift of eternal life. Think about this: Eternal life of itself is of little value. Indeed, some believe that the wicked have eternal life—only they must spend it burning in hell. To have meaning and value, the life God offers must consist of more than just a promise that you will never die. For happiness and wholeness there must be a promise of growth of accomplishment, and of responsibility. There must be the opportunity to serve and to contribute. These factors even now make life worthwhile. They are the important elements that will make eternal life meaningful too. *On these concepts mature Christianity must focus*.

The *quality* of eternal life, not the length, makes it worthwhile. At the moment we accept Christ we start building within us the capacity for truly living that will enable us to receive the most from living eternally. This progressive, positive growth-centered way of life begins at once for the person who receives salvation. But God means it to continue forever.

So, if you are a Christian, what you do and what you are, right now, are very important. Your time is now. Some people express creativity by painting pictures or writing music or poetry. And anything you create is important to you. But no matter who you are, what you yourself are becoming is in fact the most important creation of your life! You are now to allow God's Spirit within you to sculpt you into a unique, productive, and exciting representative for God.

If the crippled Antone had lived as many would expect, as an ordinary invalid, what would his life have been? Indoors most of the time, with no family and no ability to support one, he would probably have spent his days lamenting his weakness, dwelling on his infirmities, cursing his fate, pitying himself, thinking of reasons why he could not do more and be more, then die an early death.

But do not many Christians today concentrate on their sin instead on their Saviour?

Christ won the victory—for everyone. Sin need not handicap those who live in closeness to Him. He has broken its crippling, paralyzing spell, destroyed its confining power. You are free—to live triumphantly, joyfully, totally.

Instead of defeat and intimidation at the hands of his

disease, Antone threw himself into being all he could be. He did not let himself be overcome; he overcame. My boyish vision saw no crippled, twisted, defeated man. When I looked at Antone, I saw instead a strong, brave, *triumphant* man. The disease was there, but the courageous Eskimo lived powerfully and victoriously in spite of everything.

One's tendency to sin will not be totally eliminated until there is a new world. That does not mean we cannot live above it by God's grace and power right now. Christ is not coming again to forgive you your sins—to sweeten your sour temper, to suddenly make you honest, to purify your impure thoughts, to reshape your character, or to transform you into a kind and tenderhearted person. That event will remake no one's character or personality. *But if you and I have allowed God to save us right now and begin heaven in our lives and personalities right here on earth, when He comes He will simply take us home as members of the heavenly family.*

Jesus prayed for God's will to be done "in earth, as it is [done] in heaven." You and I can answer Christ's fervent prayer in our own lives. Christianity's finest hour will come as many move themselves into such oneness with God's will and God's love—as has never been done on earth before. Such oneness will carry God's family over directly from this world to the next—some without their seeing death. He will do it for you just as He did for Enoch.

4
Beyond the Conquest of Evil

How to Be More Than You Can Be

In all these things we are more than conquerors through him that loved us. Romans 8:37.

If a nation wishes to acquire prosperity, some wag once quipped, it should wage war against the United States of America and lose! More than a germ of truth animates that remark. Consider Germany and Japan. Utterly defeated in battle and ruined in economy and industry, each of these nations unconditionally surrendered to the Allies. Now West Germany and Japan are among the most economically vigorous nations on the planet and boast living standards to match.

One reason for this amazing rebound is the United States. This country began at once, with sincerity and vigor, to rebuild and restore her former enemies. America shared her wealth, skill, technology, and compassion. She guided them, giving them freedom and dignity—and the motivation and means to rebuild and grow. *She helped them to become more than they had been before.*

God does the same thing with people. Not content just to see evil removed from their lives, with His measureless resources He helps them grow into being much more than they could possibly be without Him.

My own father is not a Christian. Since he lives a

long distance away, I see him only occasionally. Our visits have always been congenial, but he has never expressed interest in spiritual things.

Since he once asked me to send him copies of anything I write, I mailed him my book *Living God's Love*, when it was published. It emphasizes the idea that God gives Christians a unique opportunity to live out His love in their lives in supernatural ways. It deals plainly with how to express love in all practical situations, even when you do not feel very loving. It talks about living in such an attitude of love that no one is capable of making you hate him, no matter what he might do to you. And it explores such concepts such as returning good for evil and living constantly in an attitude of forgiveness. Sometime after I had sent him the book, I was visiting my father. He had written no response to the book. And although I did not want to ask him what he thought about it because it was unlikely he would tell me his true feelings, I was still anxious to know. While I was out of the house, a friend along with me on the visit asked my father how he felt about the book. Later he told me that my dad had replied he had read it all, had paused a moment, then, shaking his head, had said, "But no one can love like that. Nobody can be *that* good."

In thinking about his response I came to realize that *from his viewpoint* he was right. Since he had never experienced the concepts he read about, his own experience had correctly instructed him that no one can love that well in human strength alone. By his own willpower no one can replace hostility with tenderness and understanding. A husband cannot make himself love even his own wife or his own children as God would have us love.

As the Bible says, the concepts of Christianity truly are impossible foolishness to the unbeliever. The non-Christian has no motive or capability for achieving anything beyond the level of the ordinarily human. And there can be no possibility of him, by himself, ever doing any better.

On the other hand, God is calling people—today as never before—to ready them for "naturalization" into His kingdom of heaven, to life in a different dimension. *His invitation is to a superhuman, supernatural way of life and love.* He asks, He urges, men and women to excell beyond all imaginable human capabilities at the art of living and loving. He invites you and me to not only remove any evil and sin from our lives, but to go beyond this and with His power in us *become extraordinarily kind, extraordinarily patient, extraordinarily joyful, extraordinarily creative, extraordinarily good.* By filling us with His Holy Spirit, God will infuse our human natures with the divine nature.

After he establishes his foundation on salvation by faith, the Christian next rids himself of any disobedience, any known practice of sin. He must stop consciously doing any wrong. For example, the Bible says plainly, "Let him that stole steal no more."[1]

If salvation comes so cheaply that it bears no fruit in changed behavior and philosophy, the genuineness of its reception is called into question. A superficial or verbal or even intellectual conversion—in place of a true heart conversion—may only *immunize* against the real thing. Nothing can discredit the genuine faster than the phony. *A Christianity that does not produce better people is a dangerous, deceptive counterfeit.*

Just toying with the concept of salvation by faith, as one would ponder some intellectual concept or political ideology, is perilous. And making a partial commitment or stopping at the point of justification can be exceedingly dangerous.

Had not the United States helped to rebuild West

Germany and Japan to be strong, stable nations after the war, they may easily have become engulfed by communism. An important spiritual principle applies here. A person who seeks salvation, even receives forgiveness of sin, but who fails to follow through with the rest of God's plan, is in serious trouble. When the unclean spirit is gone out of a man," Jesus warned, "he walketh through dry places, seeking rest, and findeth none. Then he saith, I will return into my house from whence I came out; and when he is come, he findeth it empty, swept, and garnished. Then goeth he and taketh with himself seven other spirits more wicked than himself, and they enter in and dwell there; and the last state of that man is worse than the first."[2]

Those who have taken some initial steps with Christianity but have never followed through on it may be manipulated by more forces of evil than previously. Remember that wars fought in the name of Christianity have always been among the most bloody and barbaric. Recall too that Christians have frequently been opposed and persecuted most often and most viciously by some of those within—or once within—their own church. Does Scripture not warn that toward the end of Earth's history, a false *religious* movement will rise up with hatred to attempt to destroy those who are true to God?

Christians must not stop short after just the conversion experience. Salvation by faith must be seen as a foundation, a launching pad, from which to move upward toward total victory over sin and selfishness.

The greatest challenge facing believers today is utilizing the promised power for living extraordinary lives, not only to uproot and eliminate evil in the life and personality, but also, to replace the vacuum with great love and great power for good. You overcome evil by your will and your surrender to God, but only through the Holy Spirit's filling is the evil replaced with something better.

A struggling but powerless religionist is a most pathetic and dangerous person. Those who "have a form of godliness, but deny the power thereof "[3] lead a life of defeat and deception. They may lay claim to a religious experience but they are lacking the power to live victoriously. Some find it impossibly difficult to keep from overeating. Some seem to lack the power to turn a television dial. Some to extinguish their final cigarette. Some to stop gossiping. And some expend huge amounts of emotional energy wrestling with temptation when, like Jacob of old, they should be wrestling with the angel of the Lord.

Many struggle to be good, to overcome evil, yet they fail and keep failing. They fail to abide in Christ. They insist on their own strength. Striving is important—but for what?—for closeness to God. God does not want merely to give us strength; He wants to give us Himself! He wants His Spirit to literally live in us, filling and overflowing the void that occurs in the life after the spirits of sin and evil are cast out. It is as the great Chinese Christian, Watchman Nee, says: *"God is not seeking a display of our Christlikeness but a manifestation of His Christ."* [4]

The greatest stronghold of evil in the world today is found not in bars and brothels of the world, the Las Vegas Strip, or Hollywood Boulevard. It is not found in the blatantly sinful lives of those who deliberately disregard God's laws. It is found rather in the lives of those who from a human viewpoint may appear to be good, *but who live without Christ. Those who try to be good by not being bad possess a counterfeit for the indwelling of the Spirit of God.* No matter how high their intentions, they manifest self instead of Christ. This is selfishness. And selfishness is the essence of sin.

The ultimate conflict between the forces of good and evil, love and selfishness, occurs not around the oil fields of the Persian Gulf or in some far-off galactic battlefield. It is happening right now in your life as the Holy Spirit of God and the evil spirit of selfishness struggle for mastery. They are not compatible. Only one can indwell.

With this indwelling of the Holy Spirit comes the next exciting dimension of the Christian experience. *It is the persistent seeking of closeness with Christ which allows the Holy Spirit to begin filling the life with the promised supernatural power.*

The presence of God is not only the total lack of sin in the life; if that were the case, we would worship only a vacuum. We recognize God as God *because of the good that He is and does!* He *deserves* our worship because of His mercy, His creativity, His loving-kindness. And when these attributes are reproduced in our characters, we come to live to be more than we in our own power can be.

Some seem to enjoy pointing with an almost gloating horror at the increase in wickedness all over the world. "See, see," they seem to chorus, "things are getting worse and worse. Christ will soon have to come and put an end to it all." They apparently assume that as soon as disaster, disease, and death reach a certain level of ugliness that their rescue will be assured. The implication is that if they sit back and wait long enough, conditions will get so bad God will *have* to do something. He will *have* to return.

The worsening conditions in the world rightly serve as a solemn reminder of the increasing pace of the conflict between good and evil. *But the inception of God's kingdom is by no means dependent on an increase of sin in the world. The fulfillment of His plans are dependent instead on the increase of righteousness in the lives and characters of His people.* It must cause God excruciating pain to see selfishness and evil increase dramatically while no parallel increase in the spiritual growth of most Christians occurs. "Your lives should be holy and dedicated to God," the Bible says, "as you wait for the Day of God, and do your best to make it come soon."[5]

As never before God is calling His people to live to be more than they can be of themselves. *A great reformation of Christianity that will sweep the church victoriously into the kingdom of God's eternal glory is here. This reformation is based on sanctification by faith in Jesus Christ through the filling of the Holy Spirit.* It is a reformation unique in human history, for it calls for Christians to become more like Jesus Christ than ever before. Not by struggle to copy Him, but by a closeness so intimate it actually allows Him to identify with them and live within them. His ways become their ways. His thoughts their thoughts. His love, theirs.

God is anxious to demonstrate to the watching universe His power not only to forgive sin but also to give victory over sin.

Satan wants no one to think that human nature can ever be perfected. His great fear is that men might discover otherwise. Thus his message has ever been "God's law is too high and holy for a human being to obey. God's character and attributes of goodness can never be reproduced in humanity. So why attempt the impossible?"

Yet around this issue the great conflict between God and Satan centers today. God plans a people living on earth right now who will show the universe that not only have they been justified and forgiven through Christ, but also sanctified and uplifted to Christlikeness through the Holy Spirit. To these people He gives the opportunity to make this history's

39

finest hour. What they allow God to do in them will prove to the universe once and for all that Satan's charges are false. Satan's charge that the law of God cannot be kept by mortals will be plainly refuted. You can imagine why the devil would be less than elated with such people! He will hurl every poisoned dart in his bitter quiver at them to discourage, destroy, and defeat. "The dragon [Satan] grew furious with the woman [God's people]" Scripture warns, "and went off to wage war on the rest of her offspring, that is, on those who keep God's Commandments and maintain their testimony to Jesus."[6]

Satan feels arrogantly content as long as he can divert Christians from the real controversy. He smiles when he sees them side-tracked on peripheral issues, even pressing social or political issues. Or, better yet, transfixed on some small point of theology. Anything that will prevent them from seeing the big picture— their role for God at this final hour. He chuckles as he watches them focus repetitiously and doubtingly on their experience of justification—babies in diapers, refusing to be weaned to solid spiritual food. Satan feels gratified that his plot to keep God's soldiers in diapers has worked so well! Can it be that down through the ages only a few have grown beyond spiritual kindergarten?

But now, the hour of the true, mature Christian soldier of the cross has arrived. Long have we been singing "Onward Christian Soldiers." Is not now the time for God's soldiers to come marching out of the worn pages of church hymnals? They must take, not only the defensive "helmet of salvation" but also the offensive "sword of the Spirit," for it is time to "put on all the armour which God provides, *so that you may be able to stand firm against the devices of the devil. For our fight is not against human foes, but against*

40

cosmic powers, against the authorities and potentates of this dark world, against the superhuman forces of evil in the heavens."[7]

With such a mighty foe, little wonder that Christians keep losing when they struggle against him under their own power. They fail to be "more than conquerors," to be more than they can be, because they fight an impossible battle.

Impossible because they strive to be good on their own, or even *with* God's assistance. The truly victorious Christian must learn to put *all* his spiritual efforts into a closeness with God. He must allow God to come *into* him, not just to support him from the outside. This Satan most fears, for this alone brings the reproduction of God's power and attributes in the human race as they were reproduced in Jesus Christ.

Think of it! God not only offers to rid evil from our lives, He also promises to fill the resulting void with His own goodness! Yes, Dad, a person can be *that* good—*if God is in him!*

5

How to Be Perfect

The Total Christian

Therefore leaving the principles of the doctrine of Christ, let us go on unto perfection. Hebrews 6:1.

One day a Christian man went out into his garden to pull weeds from the rows of lettuce growing there. Since he had been away from home on business for some weeks, the plants needed much attention. His little four-year-old daughter, delighted to have a chance to be with Daddy, followed him, eager to help. While he was stooped over, moving down a row of lettuce with his back toward her, she worked along behind. From time to time she would call out, "I love you, Daddy. I am helping you real good, Daddy."

Without looking back, the father, warmed by her affection, companionship, and willingness to help, would answer, "OK, honey. But remember to pull only the weeds."

When he finally reached the end of the row, he looked back. Stunned he discovered his faithful little helper had come along behind and uprooted a large number of plants—not weeds—lettuce!

Now do you think the father screamed, took off his belt, and began to beat her? Not this father. Realizing that his little one's feelings and intentions are more important than any number of uprooted lettuce plants, picked up his daughter, hugged her tight, and thanked her for being so helpful.

You see, this little girl is like you and me. She had perfect motives and perfect intentions. But her performance fell somewhat short of perfection![1]

Probably no religious concept has created more guilt and fear and discouragement, distracting many from the peace of salvation by faith, than perfection. That is, *a distorted concept of perfection.*

In the spiritual subconscious of some, there seems to insistently lurk the impression that somehow, some kind of personal perfection is a necessary qualification for assuring eternal life. Nothing could be further from the truth.

If you have accepted Jesus Christ as your Saviour by faith, *you are as perfect as you are going to get as far as being qualified for eternal life is concerned.* You are perfectly saved, perfectly forgiven by a perfect Saviour's perfect atonement on the cross. If you are tempted to believe that this is not enough, tempted to believe that you yourself must *still* do something to be worthy of eternal life, then you are being tempted to blaspheme God.

Satan says that what God the Father did when He gave His Son for you was not adequate. He says the cross was not sufficient to cope with *all* your sins. He tempts you to deny this—the very essence of Christianity.

The kind of perfection which qualifies you for eternal life, you already have. If you have chosen and daily continue to choose Jesus as your Saviour, His perfection stands for your imperfection. Your legal standing before God is established. He sees you as if you had never sinned. This remains true so long as you keep your life in Christ.

When the Bible uses the word *perfection*, it usually denotes spiritual growth and maturity. It should take place in every Christian's life, not in order for him to be saved, but because he has already been saved. Another word for it is *sanctification*. It simply means becoming like Jesus. Most important, it refers to loving as Jesus loved.

Notice that the Bible never speaks about perfection except in the context of loving service. Christ does call twentieth-century Christians to perfection. But it is ever a call of love. Do not fear such a call. It is a call to personal greatness, in terms not of position, but of service.

"If thou wilt be perfect," Jesus told the rich young ruler, "go and sell that thou hast, and give to the poor, and thou shalt have treasure in heaven; and come and follow me." But when this young man heard his call to *perfection*, "he went away sorrowful, for he had great possessions."[2]

Do not make his mistake and turn your back on perfection. Do not be confused and feel that it is an impossibility for you to have it, as did His disciples: "When his disciples heard it, they were exceedingly amazed, saying, Who then can be saved?"[3] Like so many today, they confused perfection with qualifying for salvation.

The answer Jesus gave the Twelve puts perfection in its proper perspective once and for all. "But Jesus beheld them, and said unto them, With men this is impossible; but with God all things are possible."[4] In His own amazing, creative way, God offers perfection to us the imperfect! What a relief that the burden for perfection does not lie on us. It lies on God.

Certainly a God who can create a world and forgive sin, provide eternal life to the redeemed, human creature, can also restore the redeemed person to His own image. God does not just put his redeemed men and women "on ice" until the arrival of the heavenly kingdom; He puts them "on fire" to light up the world with His perfect love. This is perfection. It is the ability to love and serve supernaturally.

Perfection is a lifelong growth process for the Christian. It is a journey, not a destination. It is achieved by closeness to Christ, not one's own efforts.

"Be ye therefore perfect," Jesus says, "even as your Father which is in heaven is perfect."[5] Misunderstanding this text has caused much unnecessary guilt. It is nothing more and nothing less than a call to be loving as God is loving. The immediately preceding verses challenge you to "love your enemies, and pray for those who persecute you, so that you may be sons of your Father who is in heaven; for he makes his sun to rise on the evil and on the good, and sends rain on the just and on the unjust. For if you love those who love you, what reward have you? Do not even the tax collectors do the same? And if you salute only your brethren, what more are you doing than others? Do not even the Gentiles do the same? You *therefore* must be perfect, as your heavenly Father is perfect."[6]

The word *therefore* implies a conclusion about perfection drawn from what has previously been said. Jesus has just described to His listeners on the mountainside the impartial, unfailing, unconditional love of God as it has never been described before. Then He clearly bids them to be perfect after the manner of God. That is, *by loving people as God loves people*. This is perfection in its essence.

It is *godlikeness* in its essence. It is a happy, joyous thing. Perfection—a burden for the Christian to labor under? Never! It is the kind of burden that sails are to a ship, or wings to a bird! "The fruit of the Spirit is

45

love." "The love of God is shed abroad in our hearts by the Holy Ghost,"[7] promises the Scriptures. *Spontaneous love is synonymous with real biblical perfection; it cannot be attained by an unpleasant struggle with one's own lower nature. It instead comes naturally into the character and personality as one concentrates on a life close to Christ–a life marked with the filling presence of the Holy Spirit.* God equates perfection with love because supernatural love in the life demonstrates God's presence more than the working of physical miracles.

God does not equate perfection with external behavior, such as healing the sick or speaking in tongues or even living in obedience to His laws. If external behavior were His criterion, men would begin to claim the credit, or at least to confuse what *they did* with what *God was doing. Instead, God takes His most shining gift, the gift of love, the personification of Himself, and offers it to men as their standard of perfection.* This is why Paul could so beautifully and eloquently say, "If I speak with the tongues of men and of angels, . . . if I have the gift of prophecy, and know all mysteries and all knowledge; and if I have all faith, so as to remove mountains, but do not have love, I am nothing."[8]

Could not one also say, "If I cannot speak with different tongues, if I have few supernatural gifts, if my understanding of theological matters is limited, if my faith is as small as a grain of mustard seed, yet because I have the love of God, I have *everything*?"

God views human perfection as a matter of the heart, not the "outward appearance." Like the little girl in the lettuce patch, we can have a perfect heart but a faulty understanding, perfect motives but imperfect actions. Our performance for God, yours and mine, may fall short of complete perfection from time to time. But our motives, our intentions, our goals, our dreams and desires must all be what God wants. The heart can be made perfect by Christ because He makes it His dwelling place. He fills the heart with His Spirit and His love. This brings out perfection in the present tense. "The love of God is shed abroad *in our hearts by the Holy Ghost* which is given unto us."[9] This is also the reason the Bible writer could say authoritatively, "And above all these things, put on love, which is the bond of perfectness."[10]

The call of Christians to their finest hour, the call to go beyond salvation, to go beyond the conquest of evil in the life is a call that says, "leaving the principles of the doctrine of Christ, let us go on unto perfection."[11] We know now where this call sends us—straight into the arms of the loving Father, straight into a unique, personal experience of love by the infilling of the Holy Spirit. And since, as we have seen, *sanctification* is only another word for biblical *perfection*, the Bible can recommend our "being sanctified [perfected in love], by the Holy Ghost."[12]

Sadly, because santification has not been seen its true beauty as a positive, miracle-working gift of God in the life, it has been rejected by many. Distorted concepts of perfection centering around man's own efforts have frightened the sincere away from the real thing. If perfection can be tied to salvation by works, then of course it can be discarded as a spiritual distortion. A favorite satanic strategy is to obscure the loveliness of genuine truth in an unseemly cloud of distortion and fanaticism in order to scare people away from the real thing.

A prevalent attitude today goes something like this: "Let's stay out of the spiritual dark ages. Let's be true to Reformation theology. Don't even talk about perfection. Horrors! Someone may think you are trying to work your way to heaven." This school of thought encourages Christians just to "play it safe," to presume upon their experience of justification by faith. "Christ's forgiveness is everything," they proclaim. And it is—if you understand that justification by faith gives you eternal life. But we have seen that if you stop with justification alone, you could eventually lose that very justification. There is much beyond salvation, beyond just the right to live forever. God wills you to have so much more right now as well as eternally. Jesus came, saying "The kingdom of God *is at hand*."[13] For those willing to accept more than just this first "introductory offer"—eternal life—other treasures from heaven's storehouse become abundantly available. *He offers partnership with Him in defeating evil, heavenly love, and opportunities beyond our ability even to imagine.* The people of God who have achieved closeness and oneness with Him in this life and have helped Him defeat evil in this world will be elevated to a position of joint-rulership with Christ Himself in the world to come. "Jesus Christ . . . hath made us kings and priests unto God and his Father."[14] "Do you not know that the saints shall judge the world? . . . Know ye not that we shall judge angels?"[15] "God . . . hath raised us up together, and made us sit together in heavenly places in Christ Jesus."[16]

There is much more to be accomplished in this life beyond the simple decision for salvation. This life is a great school for eternity. Here God trains the future administrators of His universe. Among all the creatures of the universe, we alone will have experienced redemption from sin and restoration to perfection.

In His parable of the men who were given the talents to invest, Jesus taught that those who are most faithful in their duties will receive the highest reward. The greater the service, the closer one draws to Him. The different degrees of responsibility and positions in heaven will be measured out according to the degree of closeness to God. To those who have been the most faithful, God will bestow the positions that involve the greatest opportunities for service in the new world. "And he that *overcometh, and keepeth my works unto the end*, to him will I give power over the nations."[17]

Thus the spiritual growth you make in your life now is an investment for all eternity. You and I are in training to take the place of the angels who fell from heaven! Angels' work has always been assisting in the administration of the government of God. Men were created "a little lower than the angels."[18] But the redeemed will find themselves elevated to a station higher than that even of the sinless Adam and Eve in the Garden. Speaking of His resurrected followers, Jesus said, "Neither can they die any more; for they are equal unto the angels; and are children of God."[19]

So let our ways now begin to become the ways of angels, not men. Let us begin to talk like the angels. To care like the angels. To love and serve like the angels. With so much to be done, with so much room to grow, can God be interested in keeping His followers "on ice" until He returns? Doesn't He rather want us "on fire" with that fire of the Holy Spirit? John the Baptist said, "He shall baptize you with the Holy Ghost, and with fire."[20]

To the church in its finest hour, the church just before Christ's return, God gives specific advice. The Laodicean church has its need addressed by the words; "I counsel thee to buy of me gold tried in the fire."[21] The gold is the gold of love. The fire is its purifying, perfecting source, the Holy Spirit. Why would this church be told it needs a genuine gift from God unless it had been accepting a counterfeit?

The counterfeit struggles to please God by becoming perfect. But those who buy it are blinded to its real nature. "Because thou sayest, I am rich, and increased with goods, and have need of nothing; and knowest not that thou are wretched, and miserable, and poor, and blind, and naked."[22]

A great search for reality, for fulfillment, for meaning is going on in both the secular and religious world today. Faced with unfulfilled lives and unsolvable problems, people are forced to become more and more aware of their true condition. The quest for personal fulfillment has spawned many television talk shows, best-selling books, school classes, sensitivity sessions, and seminars. But if you have tried "taking charge of your own life" by "pulling your own strings" or a "positive mental attitude" or if you have experimented with "winning through intimidation" by "looking out for number one" or "negotiating anything" only to discover you were still trapped in your "erroneous zones" struggling to become "your own best friend," then perhaps you are beginning to understand that man's ideas, even his best, are incapable of bringing total meaning and fulfillment to life. Man's best efforts consistently leave him mentally and spiritually incomplete. This is true in both the secular and the religious senses. Although popular psychology is not all bad, it treats only the symptoms of our human condition, not the underlying disease. It can administer a mental anesthetic for psychic suffering. But it leaves unmet the basic needs, unsolved the deepest personal problems. Falsely it teaches that in life meaning comes by direct pursuit of one's goals. One's own happiness is its illusive end.

As we have noted, the Bible teaches the exact opposite. True fulfillment, true joy, true perfection come only from wholeheartedly serving *others*. This is what Jesus did. It is success, ultimate fulfillment. There can be no higher goal or aim.

We have discussed the immense difference between good and evil, love and selfishness. The former represents the character of God; the latter forms the character of Satan. For human beings self-satisfaction has become the popular but counterfeit route to fulfillment. Unselfish love is the Christian way. John Powell has written a statement which brings this into startling perspective: "The tensions between self-fulfillment directly sought and self-fulfillment as a by-product of loving is in my judgment the greatest crisis facing men."

Both pop psychology and poor theology offer meaning and fulfillment to you by virtue of your own efforts. But you can be certain they offer the counterfeit. Regardless of the sincerity of their intentions, those who offer this kind of self-help show themselves to be Satan's marionettes, promoting the same deception he used to tempt Jesus in the wilderness: "Are you hungry? *You* can turn the stones into bread. Do you want power? *You* can rule the kingdoms of the world. Do you want perfection? *You* can achieve it—if you try hard enough and long enough."

Genuine perfection comes from no man-made scheme. One's own efforts to do more, be more, use the wrong tool for the right job. The Bible advises, "And take the helmet of salvation, and the sword of the Spirit."[23]

The helmet, a protective device, never defeated an enemy or won a battle by itself. Yet it protects the head so that the warrior can fight. Alternatively, the sword, an aggressive weapon, actively wins the victory. Likewise, the Christian's helmet of salvation protects and saves him, while his sword of the Spirit enables the warrior of God to win aggressively. And since perfection is loving service, a soldier without his sword finds himself unable to win a single battle in his spiritual life.

Focus your life, your efforts, around being continually filled with the Holy Spirit. God wants to do more than merely to fight *with* you or beside you or even to give you His strength. He wants to give you *Himself*. *He wants to live in you*. Then He can fight His battles *through* you. He can *love* through you. Thus He takes all responsibility for your accomplishments, your growth, and your perfection. What you previously considered your responsibility you now rightly see belongs to Him. It has been His all along. Perfection comes not by trying but by abiding.

"God's plan is to give us total, absolute victory twenty-four hours right now," Morris Venden writes. "Our part is to consent by opening the door day by day for continuing fellowship and communion through our choice of the private devotional life with God."[24] He asks, "Can't I have even a little bit of credit [for spiritual victory]? No. Then where should I be placing my will and willpower? Toward working on the rules, regulations, and laws for salvation? Toward the fight of sin? No. *My battle is in the area of constant relationship and dependence, in a one-to-one involvement with God.*"[25] A little further on he says, *"The greatest battle ever fought is to realize in our own minds that God is able to fulfill His promises."*[26]

After the promise of salvation, the best promise God gives (and the one unfortunately that seems most ignored today) is that of the filling of the Holy Spirit. Jesus "commanded them that they should not depart from Jerusalem, but wait for the promise of the Father, which, saith he, ye heard of me. For John truly baptized with water; but ye shall be baptized with the Holy Ghost not many days hence."[27]

God first offers salvation by faith, then the filling of

the Spirit that they may *live* as saved. "That we should be the praise of his glory, who first trusted in Christ. In whom ye also trusted, after that he heard the word of truth, the gospel of your salvation: in whom also after that ye believed, ye were sealed with that Holy Spirit of promise."[28]

Once and for all, then, perfection has absolutely nothing to do with one's own efforts. It comes strictly by choosing to allow the Spirit to live within. "There is therefore now no condemnation to them which are in Christ Jesus, who walk not after the flesh, but after the Spirit."[29]

The ultimate proof that this is where the life of victory must center has been demonstrated by Jesus. This is exactly how He achieved what He did. When He was on this earth, He did not use His own power at all. He lived victoriously by depending solely on God and the power of the Holy Spirit within Him, just as we may. He lived as we are to live so that we may overcome as He did. "I can of mine own self do nothing,"[30] He said. The extraordinary power He was given from outside Himself is available to Christians today. In fact, remarkable as it may seem, Christ actually promised that His followers would be able to accomplish even more marvelous things than He did! "Verily, verily, I say unto you, He that believeth on me, the works that I do shall he do also; and greater works than these shall he do; because I go unto my Father." And He explains the secret that makes His amazing promise a reality: "And I will pray the Father, and he shall give you another Comforter, that he may abide with you for ever; even the Spirit of truth; whom the world cannot receive, because it seeth him not, neither knoweth him: but ye know him; for he dwelleth with you, and shall be in you."[31]

Notice the intimacy that the believers will share with

the Holy Spirit. Jesus says that the Spirit will not only be *with* them but actually *in* them. Some think it would have been so grand actually to have sat at Jesus' feet, traveled with Him, eaten with Him. But do they realize they may have the Third Member of the Godhead actually living within them?

Many only experience Christ *with* them. They do not allow Him to live *in* them by the filling of His Spirit. They are less than conquerors, less than victorious in the struggle with self and selfishness. They are like the disciples before Pentecost, who walked with Jesus but were weak and powerless because they had yet to experience His radical, transforming power inside them.

Before the church's finest hour can come, a whole group of people must demonstrate the power of Jesus living *with* them. This is the key to permanent victory that Satan has been struggling to keep Christians from discovering ever since God began it at Pentecost.

Even Jesus, who was perfect and victorious, did not live by His own strength. Not even His miracles did he perform on His own. And you can live as He did and perform works as great as and even greater than His, just for the asking. When you fully realize this possibility, you can begin to see just how significant, how productive, how extraordinary your life can be right here and now! Imagine it! There is absolutely no limit to what you can do when you allow the Spirit of God to live within you! The choice is yours. You may live naturally. Or *supernaturally*.

6

I Want to See the Fire

*I indeed baptize you with water unto repentance
but he that cometh after me is mightier than I . . .
he shall baptize you with the Holy Ghost, and
with fire. Matthew 3:11.*

What if there had been no fire? On Mount Carmel
that day God was on trial. The forces of good and
evil had reached a standoff. Tension filled the air
after Baal's priests unsuccessfully attempted to attract
the attention of their god. Now it was Elijah's turn.
The altar was in place, the sacrifice animal had been
divided into parts, and everyone waited with hushed
expectancy. "How long halt ye between two opin-
ions?" Elijah asked. "If the Lord be God, follow him:
but if Baal, then follow him."

But how could the people know? Then, as now,
were the counterfeits. When a nation was caught between truth and error, Elijah came to call the devil's
hand.

"Call ye on the name of your gods," he challenged,
"and I will call on the name of the Lord: *and the God
that answereth by fire, let him be God.*"

The God that answereth by fire! It was Jehovah
versus Baal. Faith versus works. Divine strength
versus men's own efforts at holiness. Love versus self-

ishness. And the God who answered by fire was to be the one that men should serve. Will the real God please stand up? And what if there had been no fire? The priests of Baal waited. Their god had done nothing extraordinary. The people waited. The king waited. A nation waited and watched. "Lord God," the prophet prayed, "let it be known this day that thou art God in Israel, and that I am thy servant."

No one moved. Complete silence ruled the throne, with every eye riveted on the altar.

"Then the fire of the Lord fell, and consumed the burnt sacrifice, and the wood, and the stones, and the dust, and licked up the water that was in the trench." The people roared, "The Lord, he is the God; the Lord, he is the God."[1]

Today history repeats itself. Again confusion reigns over the land. Counterfeits speak boldly: "Who is God?" "What is God?" "What is truth?" "What is love?" "Can you even *really* know?" Meanwhile the church has built its altars and cut up its sacrifices as did Elijah on Carmel. But does fire light the top of the mountain? Does God answer by fire? Does no one stand before this doubting crowd? Does no one say boldly, "Let it be known this day that thou art God in Israel and that I am thy servant?" Who dares call the devil's hand? Waiting and watching this time is not merely one nation, but the whole world, indeed, the whole universe.

With so much at stake, some feel a discontent with the spiritual status quo. We love the altar, appreciate the sacrifice, and enjoy a hill on which to worship, *but we sorely miss the flame!* Today God waits to reveal Himself to the world through the fire of the Holy Spirit in the lives of His people.

Like the Baal worshipers of old, many struggle to atone for past mistakes or to appease or at least earn a bit of favor with some god. *Yet only Christ offers the very presence of God living right within.* And Christ's demonstration that He can produce better people here and now constitutes the greatest proof of Christianity's genuineness. If they are going to represent Him, God's people are going to be different, special. Specially aflame with His love, specially filled with His presence.

God gave ancient Israel something to set their religious worship apart from that of their contemporaries. God instructed Moses to build a tabernacle, a house for Him in the wilderness. What made it different from any of a thousand pagan temples? "Moses finished the work," the Bible says. "Then a cloud covered the tent of the congregation, and the glory of the Lord filled the tabernacle. . . . For the cloud of the Lord was upon the tabernacle by day, and fire was on it by night, in the sight of all the house of Israel."[2]

Not only did the pillar of fire hover over the tabernacle by night, but—and even more impressively—God's holy fire, the Shekinah, rested between the wings of the cherubim in the most holy place. It showed that the Holy Spirit was their guide. *With this mysterious gift in their midst the Israelites had the power of the Almighty God in their midst.* This was a proof, a reminder, that they were indeed to be a special, extraordinary people, fulfilled a special role in the world for God that "answereth by fire."

The Shekinah glory graces no tabernacle in the Sinai desert or temple in Jerusalem today. *It now has or seeks residence in you!* What the Shekinah was to the temple of old, the Holy Spirit is to God's temple on earth today, the committed Christian. "What? know ye not that your body is the temple of the Holy Ghost which is in you, which ye have of God, and ye are not your own?[3] *God is now filling people–not tabernacles–*

with the Holy Spirit: "Ye also are builded together for an habitation of God through the Spirit."[4]

In the darkest night of this world's sin, the "God that answereth by fire" wants to light up your life with the fire of His supernatural love. The Bible says, "The spirit of man is the candle of the Lord."[5] Here indeed is a marvelous privilege, a supreme opportunity.

When men look at your life and mine today, *do they see the fire*? Do they see something beyond the ordinary? When they look at our church today, *do they see the fire*? Do they see something more than just another building or another religious group?

Without their fiery pillar Israel would have been just another band of desert nomads. Without the fire from heaven just another disillusioned religionist chanting in front of his altar like the priests of Baal. Without the tongues of fire the apostles would have been just disbanded, discouraged, and defeated former disciples without the slightest chance of "turning the world upside down."[6] Before ascending into heaven Jesus encouraged His disciples: "Ye shall receive power, after . . . the Holy Ghost is come upon you."[7] And they did. Power enough to conquer the known world. Half an hour after Pentecost they knew more about Jesus Christ than they had learned in three years of being physically with Him. Why? Because now, through the filling of the Holy Spirit, *the truth had become an inner experience* and not merely the outer personality of Jesus. True, their Master was no longer just with them, He was *in* them. In a certain sense *He was them*. They assumed His role, His mission on earth. They were now to represent not only the truth of God but the very character and personality of God to the world. Just as Jesus did. They were to live out God's love in human terms. The Holy Spirit was the indwelling empowering agency to make this heretofore impossibility a dynamic reality. The fires of God's love were not to go out with the ascension of Christ. On the contrary, they were to light thousands of lives to burn brilliantly for Him and enlighten the whole dark world.

In history flames ignited on the Day of Pentecost have often failed to light the world because they have been few in number. Evil and darkness filled so much space they seemed to quench the fire. But, as in the time of Elijah, at least a faithful few kept the light alive. The Dark Ages of medieval times are not called dark without reason. But even then, in mountain retreats and remote valleys, the faith was kept, the torch passed.

For the followers of Christ today to be true to their heritage they must make certain—as the disciples did—that they move from having Jesus merely with them to have Him *in them*, by His Spirit. We must feel a strong discontent with merely the traditional, surface concepts of Christianity that have no power to change the heart. It is too easy to drift along, to assume that because you bear the name Christian, because your ethics are Christian, and because your behavior generally conforms to the Christian mode, you are truly living for God. Alas! You can build all these altars very carefully and very correctly, you can climb to the mountain top and cut up the sacrifice, but there you still may find no fire!

A party of French explorers in central Africa had been camped for some days in the middle of a jungle clearing. Early each morning they left for a day of exploration. Upon their return in the evening they would hurriedly gather twigs and branches to light a fire before darkness fell.

One late afternoon after coming back to camp, they discovered more than thirty carefully laid out tepeelike piles of limbs and branches. Curious, they began to take one of the piles apart. At ground level was a handful of dry leaves, over that small twigs laid crisscross, and on top of that bigger branches neatly placed. While examining this handiwork, they heard a noise behind them. Turning quickly, they glanced up into the jungle trees. There above them dozens of chimpanzees hung on the vines. The animals had watched the explorers build their fires for several days. When the men left camp that morning, the chimpanzees had come down out of the trees to try it for themselves. They had done very well indeed. The little teepees, put together with great care and effort, looked remarkably similar to those of the explorers. *But there was no fire!*

Like the chimps, many today have invested a great deal of time and concern erecting ecclesiastical teepees, theology arranged "just so." These doctrinal houses appear to be in order, carefully conforming to that of their neighbors. Their work has the "form of godliness,"[8] but denies the power. *There is no fire!*

The time has come when evil has apparently closed in again on the world. As in Elijah's time so it is now. Faith in God has almost disappeared. People show little interest in spiritual things. The line between secular and religious is so badly blurred. False gods of money and power dominate. While the people look on, confused and uncertain about the real values and real issues, the priests of the false gods chant their endless litany of self-fulfillment, secularism, science, sensuality—to name but a few. Some still search, willing to go up to the mountaintop in quest of the real God. When they do, *will they see the fire?* Will they be led to say, "The Lord, He is God"?

7

And Now I See

*He answered and said, Whether he be a sinner
or no, I know not; one thing I know, that,
whereas I was blind, now I see. John 9:25.*

I was an expert at being good once. I had gone
through Christian high school, graduated from a Christian college with a degree in theology, and spent three
years acquiring the master of divinity degree at a seminary. Then I accepted a call to a small church, and
people started calling me pastor.

Earnestly I struggled to preach like the masters of
the pulpit. I had been told once that it was necessary to
spend an hour of preparation time for every minute
that you spoke, if one wanted to preach great sermons.
Of course that took thirty hours out of my workweek
right there. But it meant preaching great sermons. In
addition I had church funds to raise, committees to
chair, flowers to take to the sick in the hospital, elderly
members to visit, backsliders to reclaim, and on and
on. I believed—and still do—that these are all worthy
tasks. And I engaged in them with a zealous intensity.

Martin Luther once said that if ever a monk could
get to heaven by his monkery, he could. Well, if ever a
pastor could get to heaven by his pastoring, I could.

With great care I maintained my orthodoxy. I kept

my morals and ethics highly polished. I coveted and received the smile of my denomination's leadership for my diligent efforts and my abounding sincerity. Pleased with my accomplishments, I indulged in but a modicum of pride, justified, I felt, by my successes. But all the while something within kept telling me I was missing a personal closeness and intimate dependence on my Saviour.

I had too many other things going—good things. My problem—it had never occurred to me that there could be such a thing as a good sinner. But that is exactly what I was. *I was trusting in my own good intentions, my own sincerity, my own dedicated service instead of Jesus Christ.*

The many good things I was doing seemed to assure me that certainly I must be pleasing God. Didn't they almost guarantee it? I mean, you couldn't be a pastor, you couldn't treat your wife well, and you couldn't have people tell you what wonderful sermons you preached if you weren't right with God, could you?

Then one day the church conference president called me on the phone. "We are promoting you to a larger church," he said. That, of course, stood as a proof of my spiritual "good and regular" standing.

But God is gracious. He did not give up on me. He loves "good" sinners as well as "bad." In His own time and in His own quiet, unexpected ways, our Father keeps trying to reach each of us with spiritual reality.

He reached me after the birth of our first child, our son. My wife had spent two days and nights in the hospital. When she arrived back home, I, thinking myself kind, generous, and helpful, volunteered to take care of the baby the first night so my wife could get some much-needed sleep.

Baby woke me up at midnight, whimpering. Immediately I hurried out of bed and did my best to soothe him, feeling very tender and fatherly. He soon drifted off again, and with a sigh of satisfaction I went back to bed. At one a.m. Baby woke me up again bawling loudly. I struggled out of bed, tripped over my own slippers, and staggered down the hall to his basinette. This time my infant seemed determined not to be silenced. I followed my wife's instructions on feeding very carefully—to no effect. But with extensive back-patting and floor-pacing I finally hushed him back to sleep. And with a sigh of relief I tucked the covers around him. I crawled back into bed, flicked out the light, and as I slipped off to sleep, I remember thinking how virtuous it was of me to be doing something many fathers would not consider.

But at two a.m. Baby Cooper's piercing wails roused me out of semi-consciousness. Groaning, I dragged myself to his side. His much more violent protests I discovered much to my horror were due to the fact that nature had taken its relentless course. So, squinting as I attempted to adjust my eyes to the bedside light, and totally without feminine support or supervision, I began my first solo attempt at diaper changing.

My child was most impatient and unsympathetic with my technique. He wriggled and screamed horribly through it all. Even after the ordeal was over he seemed determined to rehash everything with great lungfulls of noisy air. Not even a warm bottle could still his howls. Again I paced the floor of the small apartment with my bundle. This time for half an hour before at last my boy had finished telling all to the world.

Back in bed and thinking seriously of closing and locking the bedroom door and burying my head under my pillow, I fell immediately to sleep.

Baby's timing was perfect. At close to three a.m. he struck again. This time, my patience exhausted, I catapulted off the bed, flew down the hall, snatched my child from his crib, and began angrily stalking the living-room floor. As he continued to wail, I clutched him tighter and tighter, irritation growing into a hostility I never realized I possessed. I found myself starting to shake the baby to make him stop crying.

At that point it hit me—what kind of person was I anyway? What sort of monster inside me could prompt such resentment and rage toward my own helpless, innocent, newborn son?

What I discovered about myself that night shook me. From that revealing experience and others like it, I finally began to learn something about my own nature. I found that I—I of the finely polished and professional outward exterior, I of the abundant good works, I of the properly correct theology and the "great" sermons—I on the inside was indeed selfish and hostile and unloving.

Under a true challenge my carefully practiced love had evaporated like dew before summer sun. I could not even unselfishly love my very own innocent, baby son. I was in fact wretched, poor, blind, and naked. I, the expert at being good, who had been so sure that I "had need of nothing," had discovered myself to be a sinner in the first degree.[1] My life had substituted many fine concepts, goals, and good deeds in place of a total dependence on Jesus. My kind of goodness was never more than a veneer that when finally scratched revealed an ugly truth.

I saw at last I could never hope to fill my inner needs myself. I realized at last that Douglas Cooper could not do it his way. I had to admit my "good" was not good enough. I needed to have a Saviour to depend on *for this life as well as for the eternal.*

I did not just need Christ *with* me. I had had that for years. I needed Jesus *in* me. I needed the kind of love that would last from two a.m. to four a.m. The unconditional kind that only His Holy Spirit can give, that would take over when my meager, human supply was exhausted. If I was even going to love my own wife and child well—not to mention others who were not as close, and whom I might in fact find unappealing and unlovable—I needed Christ's supernatural patience, too, as well as an abundance of His wisdom and goodness.

God had finally crossed the frigid channel of my own self-sufficiency, exposed my great unworthiness—the part of me I had always masked from others and even myself—and had established a personal beachhead in my life on the point of my greatest need.

God caused lasting change in me. He gave me the assurance of my salvation, and I received the true fulfillment and peace that comes from knowing that if Christ should come immediately, or I should die tomorrow, by His grace I would have eternal life. This kind of assurance could never be mine as long as I continued to assume that I had *some personal part* in qualifying. Deep down I always knew I could not do it by myself—but self wanted the good things I was doing to earn me at least a little bit of credit!

I learned that only when I let Jesus "do it all" that He can "save to the uttermost."[2] At last I was able to let Him do it for me. It seems I had trusted in everything religious—but Him. I had always thought I received salvation through the Bible. That was a real trap because I had automatically assumed I had salvation because I believed in the Bible. Hadn't I spent years studying it, even in the original languages of Hebrew and Greek? I had yet to learn that love letters are not the ultimate end of courtship. Marriage is. Even the Bible is *not* to be the center of Christianity. Jesus Christ is. After many years I had finally learned it is not merely inspired words that nourish the soul—it is God Himself. As A. W. Tozer has written, "The modern scientist has lost God amid the wonders of His world; we Christians are in real danger of losing God amid the wonders of His Word."[3]

Once I had assumed that being a "great theologian might be the sure way to God. At last God showed me that Satan is the best theologian the world has ever seen. My dictionary says that theology is the "science dealing with God and His relationship to the universe." Lucifer was and is past master of it. The understanding of even the finest truth, the comprehension with the intellect of spiritual knowledge, as important as this may be, makes no one a genuine Christian. This is why Paul could say with such eloquence and meaning that though he might "understand all mysteries, and all knowledge" if he did not possess the love that comes from a personal encounter with God, he had nothing.[4] The world and the church do not so much need more great Bible scholars and theologians today nearly so badly as they need more Spirit-filled, loving, caring, sharing Christians.

My theology, my church had always been the center of my spiritual life before. Now Christ took that position. I had always thought that the gospel was a great body of truth, a great message, or a great church movement. I learned that it is nothing without a great Person—Jesus Christ Himself. Without Him living within me, my theology was only another brand of egotism, speculative philosophy. Without Him, my Christian ministering was just another sort of social service.

Jesus Christ did not come to this world primarily to preach a message. *He came to be the message*. He is Himself Christianity.

When I made this conscious choice for Christ over other spiritual things, Christ over self, Christ over custom and convention and convenience, He became at last free to share His eternal life with me. *He became free to infuse His very own nature and personality into me by His Spirit.*

Some months after personally beginning to experience salvation by faith, God began nudging me toward another important dimension of Christianity. In my new relationship my personal, basic spiritual needs were being met as never before. Almost content to enjoy this experience until the Lord came, yet I sensed a need for something more. I began to see that God wanted me to be and do more for Him. But this time I wanted to fill this need with the right motives and the right power.

Living in Christ now was letting Him help me to grow away from my selfishness and my negative traits. At this time the " bad things" were not bothering me, but I began to feel frustrated about not being able to do greater good. I wanted my life to count for more—to speak with greater power, to write with greater wisdom, to listen to others with more compassion. I felt that the Bible studies I gave, the sermons I preached, the words I wrote were not producing the fruit they should. They seemed to me to lack some kind of impact. Besides, though still relatively young, I sensed that my life was quickly slipping by. Life was too precious to live a minute of it in an ordinary manner, and I seemed to be doing that too much of the time. I was restless. I wanted extraordinary results. But my own talents and knowledge were not sufficient. I wanted extraordinary fellowship with other Christians. I wanted to see and experience and to be able to share extraordinary joy and love every day.

In my years of studying the Bible I had learned of

the doctrine of the Holy Spirit, including the concept of the filling of the Holy Spirit. I of course had always assumed that I automatically qualified. After all, remember me? The one who had studied theology on both the undergraduate and graduate levels? Who had given his life to God's work? Who had made such honest and successful attempts to be good? After all, if salvation was mine, wasn't the Holy Spirit rightly mine as well? Hadn't I been truly converted to Christ? Had not the Holy Spirit been working on my heart?

Indeed He had, but for a long time I had not seen the gigantic difference between the Spirit's external work drawing a person to God and His internal work, *filling* a person and *living in him*. The Holy Spirit's work of drawing people to their heavenly Father must never be confused with His work of filling those who respond. I had mistakenly assumed that because the Spirit had been guiding or attempting to guide me throughout my life, that I was filled with the Holy Spirit.

I developed a hunger to learn everything I could about the Spirit. I began to pore over the Bible searching for everything it said on the subject. I preached my first sermon on the Spirit. I read every book I could find on the topic.

Yet as I studied I began to fear that any interest I might show in the filling of the Holy Spirit would be branded immediately as sympathy for, if not outright defection to, the ranks of the charismatic movement. In some church circles even mentioning the term "the baptism of the Spirit" could cause the raising of ecclesiastical eyebrows. It could provide instant reaction and admonition about "fanaticism" and possession by the wrong kind of spirit. But at the same time I became impressed that while there was a counterfeit for every good and godly thing, nonetheless this could be all the more proof the genuine really was there. Satan's counterfeit made the real thing seem all the more worth looking into.

The more I learned about the filling of the Holy Spirit, the more I became convinced *that it is a separate, spiritual experience offered after conversion to every Christian* and initiated by the baptism of the Holy Spirit. Certain that I did not have it, I was just as certain that I wanted it.

I realized that through this special spiritual gift Christ empowered believers and equipped them for a ministry to the world. I came to see it as a gift far beyond what natural abilities, talents, and education could produce. I discovered that it comes just as simply and naturally as any of God's gifts, including salvation, that I could have it merely for the asking. I did not yet have it, only because I had not yet asked for it. "Ye have not, because ye ask not."[5] I came to understand the receiving of the filling of the Holy Spirit as a simple act of faith. All that is necessary is faith, nothing more. For the Bible says "we might receive the promise of the Spirit through faith."[6] This text became the key.

Not long after reaching this level of understanding I knew the time had come for me to ask. From further Bible study I found that God had set up an order for administering the Spirit. The Scriptures associate it with requests in an atmosphere of prayer involving another person or persons. I should not attempt to seek the gift strictly by myself. On the other hand, "He [Jesus] shall baptize you with the Holy Ghost,"[7] says the Scripture. Thus no man could claim credit for baptizing another with the Holy Spirit, yet in His wisdom God had seen fit to make the experience more meaningful and confirming by allowing others to participate. The Bible example is followed most closely when a fellow Christian, himself Spirit-filled, lays his hands on the head of the receiver and joins him in his prayer requesting this precious gift from on high. Most New Testament seekers received the gift in this manner. (The Bible does mention exceptions, when this simple procedure was *not* requisite, especially during the first few tumultuous days following Pentecost. After more order had been established, however, almost without exception the laying on of hands was carried out whenever Christians were baptized with the Holy Spirit.)

Realizing this and wishing to be as true to the biblical pattern as possible, I traveled some distance to share in the experience of asking and receiving with a man I was certain had experienced the filling of the Spirit. This man never boasted of this, claimed he had received the blessing because of his own piety, or even believed that having received it he had become spiritually superior. Yet his dynamic, healthy, positive, trusting certainty that God had provided this great gift for him, his life of victory and power, and his special kind of ministry indicated to me that something this special had truly occurred in his life.

As he laid hands on my head and quietly prayed, I was impressed that I was indeed taking another step in God's will for me. Without doubt, needs I felt were being met. No electrical pulse surged through me, no lights flashed from the sky, no speaking in tongues burst from my lips. But I felt a calm, assuring joy, a depth of love and tenderness for God in my heart unlike anything I had ever felt before.

I came away from that special time with the assurance that indeed I was now baptized with the Spirit. Not because I had worked hard enough to scour enough sin out of my life to make myself worthy at last. Nor because I had experienced some ecstatic experience, for I had not. A single reason convinced me that

I had received: *God had promised and I had asked.* God does not lie. He who had said that upon my request in faith He would eagerly give me this great gift had simply done so.

My faith was confirmed by what began to follow. I received almost immediately an even more profound hunger for the Bible and joy in reading and *absorbing* it. The Scriptures became even more special to me. I had a unique feeling of great wealth in possessing them. I bought a cassette tape deck and put it in my car so I could listen to recorded readings of the Bible as I drove. I typed out important verses of Scripture that had personal meaning and taped these to various walls around my house so I could more easily memorize them. When time to do other things arrived, I found myself only reluctantly laying aside the Bible. I had *never* felt this way before. Previously I had studied to prepare for classes, to make up my "great sermons," to indoctrinate others, or out of a sense of duty or need. Now I read for sheer delight.

Someone introduced me to conversational prayer. Being a rather private person, I had previously found prayer in groups unenjoyable. Now it became one of my greatest blessings and joys, literally highlighting my spiritual life along with fellowshiping and sharing in small Christian groups. Here I tapped into vital living currents of spiritual prayer and love I had never before known. *I learned that if believers are willing to create an atmosphere of oneness, trust, love, and commitment to Jesus among themselves in a small group, the Holy Spirit will never fail to join them and touch their lives—deeply and healingly.* I became able to "confess my faults" to others as the Bible admonishes,. [8] My spiritual egotism shrank, and I began to feel compassion.

Other changes occurred. People began responding.

Since God gives His Spirit primarily for service to others, I found that people seemed to listen in a new way now to what I was saying when I preached. When I counseled, I sensed for the first time that I was beginning to reach beyond mere clever psychological insights, "band-aid" ministry, or textbook answers. I felt a new sense of purpose as I realized I was starting to meet real and deep needs.

I was able to begin boldly doing things for God I never would have dared to attempt when I was operating on my own spiritual batteries. One of them was leaving the paid pastoral work. I moved my family to a distant place where there was no church to raise up a body of believers.

In terms of human logic, this decision appeared irrational. Older pastors warned me—I was "throwing away my future." Educated in theology, I had no apparent means to support my family. We knew not a single person in the new area. Concerned parents, fearful that I might have lost my reason and convinced that I would be subjecting their grandchildren to eventual malnourishment as well as physical and emotional deprivation, pleaded with me. But my wife, to her everlasting credit and to my extreme amazement, raised no objection. For myself, from the beginning I knew I was being led. I had assurance, confidence, and peace.

It proved to be the greatest adventure so far in our lives. Within three years, where there had been nothing before, there stood a beautiful new church with a warm, enthusiastic congregation. And yet very little of this success came about because of my own efforts. At times it seemed to occur in spite of them. My chief role seemed to be in asking, then stepping back out of the way to watch the Lord provide.

In my study, I had learned something else exciting about this gift of the Holy Spirit. To everyone who asks for the baptism, God seems to give an extra spiritual gift, something beyond themselves and their own abilities. It is a special endowment of reaching out with God's love to others in unique, productive ways.

Though I had previously published a few articles in secular magazines, I had never done any serious Christian writing. But since my baptism of the Holy Spirit I had learned that people's lives could be warmed and touched in ways I had never before witnessed, I discovered that God wanted me to write for Him as well. My ministry could widen so that the Holy Spirit could work through me in sharing insights and concepts that could never have come from my own reasoning or my own literary effort. He could be a wonderful creative force. I began to write and publish articles and books telling others what the Holy Spirit was doing within me.

I firmly believe that any Christian can truly have this special dimension of spiritual life without participating in the charismatic movement, without speaking in tongues, without some ecstatic emotional experience. This has been the most satisfying discovery I have ever made. But I was able to receive it only *after* I discovered personally from the Bible that the baptism of the Spirit is a *distinct, separate, personal, spiritual experience beyond salvation that must be specifically sought out and requested by faith before it can be received.* I am convinced it can *never* become a reality from my own personal experience that simply because you happen to be a Christian or because the Holy Spirit has been working on you, as He does even non-Christians.

I found that the baptism of the Spirit is available most genuinely when requested by faith—the simple, straightforward, biblical method. But I do not believe I was given a ''once Spirit-baptized always Spirit-baptized" experience. No one is. It is just as possible to lose the Spirit as it is to lose salvation. God does not remove our freedom with this experience. Being filled with the Spirit is also a daily matter. What I did receive on that special day became the foundation upon which the daily receiving—stone by "living stone"[9]—could become a temple for God's Shekinah.

The laying on of hands must never be seen as a magical shortcut to sanctification. Perfection is a lifelong journey, not a destination instantly reached.

Such baptism makes no one better or superior to anyone else. Nor does it make anyone sinless. However, when you do make a mistake you will tend to be much more painfully aware of it. You will be disappointed many times when you find yourself slipping back into doing things by your own volition. You will enjoy new dimension in your spiritual life—what it is to live, work, act, and talk, *in the Spirit* as compared with the same activity you previously performed *out of the Spirit*. As time goes on, you will find you keep yourself more and more in the Spirit because you simply cannot afford the alternative! You will discover that you are truly a different person when you seek the filling of the Spirit each day. You will walk differently, treat others differently, use your time differently.

You will find Christ much more real and precious to you than ever before. You will experience a sense of confirmation, a reality about spiritual things that will banish doubts. You will view life in a totally new perspective. You will receive amazing insights into people and ideas that you will recognize did not originate in your own intellect. You will experience the fruits of the Spirit—the love, joy, and peace—becoming more and more infused naturally into your life. You will discover yourself intrigued with ideas and concepts that once held no concern, while other things that have tended to take your time and devotion away from Christ will start to lose their appeal. You will become a different person, a "new creation."[10]

To one man who received the Spirit, it was promised, "And the Spirit of the Lord will come upon thee, and thou shalt prophecy with them, and *shalt be turned into another man*. . . . God gave him another heart."[11]

More than anything else you could possibly conceive of, it is God's own special way of making every hour of your life your finest.

8

The Divine Imperative

Be filled with the Spirit.
Ephesians 5:18.

Some historians claim that Western civilization owes more to the great evangelist John Wesley and his companions than to any other group. Some describe him as having the brains of a scholar and the tongue of an orator. The first years of his professional life, as he attempted to teach and preach, were frustrating to him however. He was converted, he says, but he still sensed a great lack in his life. He was able to bring his words and actions into harmony with God, but he had a terrific struggle with his thoughts. He lacked confidence and strength and felt insecure. He knew his preaching was powerless because there was so little response to it.

Fearful at his own spiritual weakness, disillusioned and dejected, he became acquainted with a group of Spirit-filled Christians who helped him to change his life remarkably. He described one of their services, which showed a striking contrast to the lifeless formalism burdening the services of the Church of England. "The great simplicity as well as solemnity of the whole," he wrote, "almost made me forget the seventeen-hundred years between and imagine myself in one of those assemblies where form and state were not: but Paul the tentmaker, or Peter, the fisherman presided, yet with the demonstration of the Spirit and power."

Wesley decided to seek the filling of the Spirit for himself. At another meeting he heard a statement read from Luther describing the inner change the Spirit can work on the heart of the believer. At this meeting John Wesley was baptized with the Spirit. He tells of experiencing what was a new dimension of spiritual life. "I felt my heart strangely warmed," he said.

Wesley came away with a new vision, a new passion, new power. Virtually unheard of before this time, his preaching went on to shake three nations. He moved through the British Isles like a firebrand, turning a nation from its dry, formal, powerless religion to a dynamic encounter with God.

He and his followers led in the reform of not only the church but of society as a whole. They implemented drastic and badly needed prison reforms, championed the dignity of man, and promoted civil and human rights. Prohibited from preaching in the churches and banned from the cities, they preached in the fields. Thousands climbed to the top of the London wall to hear this Spirit-filled man of God.

Every Christian receives the same power to do great things for God. Satan desires above all else to keep this experience away from every believer. The apostle Paul, who probably had done more to disrupt the work of evil and advance the cause of the kingdom of God on earth than any other man who has ever lived, could say with assurance at the end of his Spirit-filled life, "I have fought a good fight."[1] And every devil had to agree!

The Christian who has not sought the baptism of the Spirit presents no threat to the forces of evil. *In fact, if Satan can prevent enough Christians from being baptized with the Spirit, he can postpone the second coming of Christ indefinitely!* The filling of the Spirit moves one from the ranks of the comfortable, conforming churchgoer, placidly awaiting the hope of a future heavenly reward "someday," and transforms him into a dynamic warrior for God. One who gives his all to building up the kingdom of God right now.

In these last vital hours of earth's history, such an immensely important spiritual experience as the baptism of the Holy Spirit is no luxury, no mere optional alternative for the Christian. It is not something you can just assume will come to you someday, something you can take or leave depending on spiritual taste and social preference. The Bible says positively, "Be filled with the Spirit."[2]

"Christians are as guilty for not being filled with the Spirit as sinners are for not repenting," Charles G. Finney said. "They are even more so, as they have more light, they are so much the more guilty."

"Receive ye the Holy Ghost,"[3] Christ Himself commanded. He also warned a man who was already committed to God, a man who was already leading a good, moral life, by stating, "Verily, verily I say unto thee, Except a man be born of water *and of the Spirit*, he cannot enter into the kingdom of God."[4]

Clearly, then, conversion and forgiveness of sins, for which being "born of water" is a symbol, is not all there is to the total, victorious Christian life. How diligently through the centuries the powers of evil have conspired to keep believers away from that "something more"—the filling of the Spirit.

I have to take a deep breath every time I repeat it, its implications are so great, but I cannot agree more with Catherine Marshall when she says, "Any church that ignores the Spirit is an apostate church."[5] Ignoring this source of ultimate spiritual power, ignoring this last promise of Christ, ignoring this Divine Being, Heaven's specially given link with mankind is indeed the worst kind of blasphemy. The ultimate insult, even in human circles is to ignore someone, to pretend he or she does not exist. It can have an effect worse than hatred, because hatred at least recognizes the existence of the hated one and his importance by the force of its negative action. Even God prefers the spiritually cold, those who are openly against Him, to the neutral, the spiritually lukewarm.

The fact that many questions about the Holy Spirit are unanswerable does not supply ground for ignoring Him. His existence and abilities defy human logic. They cannot be fully explained. Yet the Holy Spirit is made all the more significant and meaningful precisely because the mystery cannot be grasped by mere human reason, for our God is bigger than we are.

Apply the finest of human reason, collect all the multitude of relevant Bible texts, and you still will not necessarily be convinced of the reality of the baptism of the Holy Spirit. The convincing comes only in the experiencing. The simple step of faith does it. Jesus said, *Do and you will know*. "If any man will *do* his will, he *shall know* of the doctrine, whether it be of God, or whether I speak of myself."[6] A spiritual reality becomes certain not so much by studying or dialoguing as by personal trial.

The blind man who was healed by Jesus could not intellectually explain what had happened to him. He did not even know for sure who Jesus was. When the Pharisees challenged the reality of his experience by casting doubt on it and on Jesus, he said, "Whether [Jesus] be a sinner, or no, I know not: one thing I know, that, whereas I was blind, *now I see*."[7] Because he had experienced Him personally.

His can be your joyous testimony. As the indwelling presence of the majestic Third Person of the Godhead opens your spiritual eyes to the vision of life and love and power you never knew could exist, you also can say with confidence, "One thing I know, that, whereas I was blind, now I see."

Just as the self-righteous Pharisees would deny the blind man even the validity of his physical healing, so many would deny you anything beyond the ordinary blindness of their idea of what your spiritual life should be. Here great spiritual battles will soon be fought; here is the growing edge in spiritual advancement.

The filling of the Spirit is not just another sermon topic touched on once a year, not only an item in a list of church doctrines on the back of a church bulletin, not simply something to be strung up on a banner at a church convention to be taken down, rolled up, and forgotten about as soon as the last bus leaves. It is rather *spiritual dynamite*.

Why? I summarize four reason: (1) It maintains your saved condition daily. (2) It empowers your Christian life so that sin will not only be *forgiven* but also gradually *overcome*—in your life! (3) It prepares you to live in the atmosphere of heaven by infusing divine characteristics and personality into your life. (4) It gives you a unique and truly fruitful ministry to the world.

This is no "spiritual self-help device." Regardless of the earnestness and sincerity involved, such humanly engineered programs can at best but imitate godly behavior and correct beliefs. The genuine article comes only through the indwelling of the Holy Spirit.

"It is impossible for any Christian to be effective either in his life or in his service," writes Henrietta C. Meras, "unless he is filled with the Holy Spirit who is God's only provision of power."

In a parable a man had been entrusted by his master with a talent, *a special gift*, something with great potential. Unfortunately *he decided to bury it in the ground*. He ignored its great power for good. When the lord returned, he did not excoriate the servant for no longer believing in him or for any evil practices, but for the great good the man had decided not to do. He condemned him because he had abused his master's great gift: He branded him a "wicked and slothful servant," then instructed others, "Cast ye the unprofitable servant into outer darkness [where] there shall be weeping and gnashing of teeth."[8]

When Christ ascended to heaven, He offered you His Holy Spirit, His best gift for service to Him and others. Have you buried it? Do not ignore and thus reject the gift of the baptism of the Holy Spirit and thus ignore and reject the Lord who intrusts it to you.

"Ye are not in the flesh, but in the Spirit, if so, be that the Spirit of God *dwell in you*. Now if any man have not the Spirit of Christ, *he is none of his*."[9]

Without this gift, Christ's sacrifice on the cross would have been in vain. For sin can be overcome in the life only through the mighty agency of the Holy Spirit. The Spirit thus makes Christ's accomplishment on the cross effectual for Christians. "We want our transitory life to be absorbed into the life that is eternal," the apostle Paul explained. "Now the power that has planned this experience for us is God, and he has given us his Spirit as a guarantee of its truth."[10] The baptism of the Spirit is a "guarantee," a confirming experience of salvation. "In him you also, who have heard the word of truth, the gospel of your salvation, and have believed in him, were sealed with the promised Holy Spirit, which is the guarantee of our inheritance until we acquire possession of it, to the praise of his glory."[11] The Spirit works with Christ to make salvation a blessed reality in the ongoing life of the victorious Christian. "But ye are washed, but ye are sanctified, but ye are justified in the name of the Lord Jesus, and by the Spirit of our God."[12]

The baptism of the Spirit, essential for faithfulness to Christ as the Saviour, is also essential for effective service. The disciples who had been with Jesus knew their commission to take the gospel to the world, but— before they received the power of the Spirit—quickly abandoned that commission and went back to their old occupations. "I go a fishing," said Simon Peter. "We also go with thee," chimed in others.[13]

Unless their conversion is followed by the filling of the Spirit, converted Christians, like these disciples, tend to drift back into their old habits and practices. Not that there is anything wrong with commercial fishing! But if the believers do not move from the spiritual positon of "being *with*" Christ to that of "having Him indwell" them by the Spirit, they may waste their life on activities not spiritually essential. Eventually they may find themselves in the position of the servant who but buried his master's talent.

Until the fire of the Spirit fell on the disciples, they had no vision, no power, no motivation. Little wonder Jesus saw them as unready to serve. "I send the promise of my Father [the Holy Spirit] upon you," He cautioned them. "But tarry ye in the city of Jerusalem, until ye be endued with power from on high."[14]

In spite of all the *time* they had spent with Christ and all the *knowledge* they learned about Him in three years, until Pentecost they *lacked the power*.

How futile for them to have attempted to achieve any spiritual work in their own strength! Outward religion without the inward presence of the Spirit can be very unattractive and even counterproductive. As Watchman Nee writes, "We have to learn the lesson of not doing—of keeping quiet for Him. We have to learn that if God does not move we dare not move. . . . We dare not act, we dare not speak, except in conscious and continual dependence on Him."[15]

Christ Himself was so totally dependent on the leading of the Holy Spirit that He made no plans for Himself. He took each day as it came and accepted God's guidance for Him for that day. We should too. "Not by might, nor by power, but by my spirit, saith the Lord of hosts."[16]

"The church without power is a factory for hypocrites," well-known Christian pastor Samuel Shoemaker said.[17] And evangelist Charles Spurgeon spoke even more strongly: "If we do not have the Spirit of God, it were better to shut up the churches, to nail up the doors, to put a black cross on them and say, 'God have mercy on us.' If your ministers have not the Spirit of God you had better not preach, and your people had better stay at home. I think I speak not too strongly when I say that a church in the land without the Spirit of God is rather a curse than a blessing."

9

The Promised Power

A man full of faith and of the Holy Ghost.
Acts 6:5.

Dwight L. Moody—in my mind the name calls up images of vast crowds gathered to listen earnestly to the great Christ-centered preaching of this mighty man of God. But he had not always such power.

A Christian preacher for years, Moody once experienced an earnest yearning for the filling of the Holy Spirit. He began to feel that unless he could receive this gift he wanted to preach no more. During this time, the city of Chicago, where Moody's headquarters were, experienced its most destructive fire. Moody went to New York to help raise money for the rebuilding of the city. But something else was on his mind. "My heart," he confided later to his son, "was not in the work of begging. . . . I could not appeal. I was crying all the time that God would fill me with His Spirit. Well, one day, in the city of New York—oh, what a day!—I cannot describe it, I seldom refer to it; it is almost too sacred an experience to name. Paul had an experience of which he never spoke for fourteen years. I can only say that God revealed Himself to me, and I had such an experience of His love that I had to ask Him to stay His hand. I went to preaching again. The sermons were not different; I did not present any new truths, and yet hundreds were converted. I would not now be placed back where I was before that blessed experience if you could give me all the world—it would be as the small dust of the balance.''[1]

When she was one year old, my daughter received her first Christmas present. So thrilled was she with the colorful outer wrapping that she refused to open it. She wanted to keep the gift just the way it was. Christ has given the "present" of the Holy Spirit to every follower. But unless "opened," the present will do nothing.

The two most vital and overlooked truths about the baptism of the Holy Spirit are these: (1) It is a separate and distinct dimension of spiritual life which must be personally sought and appropriated after conversion, and (2) it is given primarily to empower the believer for a personal, unique, supernatural ministry to others *when they are ready to begin a service to the world.*

Have you ever wondered why Jesus had no public ministry—did no evangelism, recruited no disciples, and worked no miracles—for the first thirty years of His life? During these quiet years at Nazareth, He worked as a carpenter, made baby cribs, perhaps, and dining-table chairs. Surely He got shavings in His sandals and slivers in His fingers. Aside from the fact that He studied the Scriptures keenly and maintained a powerful communion with God, His life in many other respects was little different from that of the average person of His time and place.

The Holy Spirit—though instrumental in His conception, protection, guidance, and instruction—had as yet not filled Jesus with the fullness of His mighty power. Then, after His water baptism by John, the Holy Spirit "came upon" Him.

This infilling changed His life. No longer just the carpenter from Nazareth, He was now the Messiah, a man with a ministry, a mission. *Jesus needed the power of the Holy Spirit to accomplish His special work for God and to do His miracles. Not even Jesus Christ worked by His own power, but by the power of the Spirit.* Incredible as it may seem, you and I need that same power—and for the same purpose. We need that same Presence to accomplish anything beyond the human level.

Jesus Christ, even when on earth, had a divine nature *of His own equal* to the Father's and the Holy Spirit's. *But He did not use it.* Thus He demonstrated to you and me the great power God shares with us when we allow His Holy Spirit to possess us as Christ did.

The Bible tells us that after Christ returned to heaven, He shared the Holy Spirit with His followers. "Ye men of Israel, hear these words; Jesus of Nazareth, a man approved of God among you by miracles and wonders and signs which God did by him in the midst of you, as ye yourselves also know. . . . Therefore being by the right hand of God exalted, and having received of the Father the promise of the Holy Ghost, he hath shed forth this, which ye now see and hear."[2]

As we have seen, Christ told His disciples they would accomplish even greater works with the Spirit's power than His own miracles. "Verily, verily, I say unto you, He that believeth on me, the works that I do he shall do also; and greater works than these shall he do; because I go unto my Father."[3] When you stop to think about it, you realize that the disciples did practically everything supernatural that Jesus had done within just a few years after His ascension. They raised the dead (Acts 9:36-42), read minds (Acts 5:3), vanished (Acts 8:39), healed, cast out devils.[4]

Whether of Jesus or His disciples, all miracles were accomplished through the power of the Holy Spirit. For, as Jesus said, "I can of mine own self do nothing."[5]

Scripture details many events which show Jesus under the control of the Holy Spirit. "And Jesus, being full of the Holy Ghost returned from Jordan, *and was led by the Spirit* into the wilderness." When His time of testing in the desert was over, "*Jesus returned in the power of the Spirit* into Galilee; and there went out a fame of him through all the region round about." *The Spirit of the Lord is upon me*," He proclaimed, "because he hath anointed me to preach the gospel to the poor; he hath sent me to heal the brokenhearted, to preach deliverance to the captives, and recovering of sight to the blind, to set at liberty them that are bruised."[6]

If Jesus Christ, who was sinless and perfect and in complete communion with God, had to wait thirty years until He was ready to use the Spirit's power for witness and ministry as a distinct, special gift from heaven, then surely we must never presume we have received it in our lives merely because we are Christians and happen to be trying to lead moral, orderly lives. If Jesus waited until He was ready to begin service, should not His followers do likewise? The baptism of the Spirit, while blessing the recipient, is primarily a distinct equipping for supernatural *service*.

After he had been filled with the Spirit, Dwight L. Moody wrote: "In some sense and to some extent the Holy Spirit dwells in every believer, but there is another gift which may be called the gift of the Holy Spirit for service. This gift, it strikes me, is entirely distinct and separate from conversion and assurance."

Bible accounts of believers receiving the Spirit usually bear out these conclusions: (1) The receivers were converted before being filled with the Spirit but lacked power and/or victory in their lives. (2) Receiving the Spirit was a separate experience from conversion. After receiving the gift, they began to work wondrously for God.

Peter, not many days after he had returned to his fishing nets in discouragement, was transformed and infused at Pentecost. He was soon preaching sermons with unimaginable power. Thousands were converted. The Scriptures described him as "Peter, filled with the Holy Ghost."[7]

Stephen, "a man full of faith and of the Holy Ghost,"[8] appointed a deacon by disciples underestimating the effect Spirit-filling can have, humbly took care of church finances and widows and orphans. But the power of the Holy Spirit within him burst through these behind-the-scenes activities!

His Spirit-directed words and deeds soon got him into trouble. The Jewish leaders seized Stephen and brought him before the Sanhedrin. Stephen eloquently defended himself against the charges brought against him. But his powerful, to-the-point defense infuriated them, for he said, "Ye stiffnecked and uncircumcised in heart and ears, *ye do always resist the Holy Ghost*: as your fathers did, so do ye."[9]

This was too pointed a comment for them. Infuriated they picked up stones to hurl at him. They wanted to end his life.

Stephen did not chide them for not *believing in* the Spirit, but for ignoring Him, resisting His power, His presence, and His desire to fill their lives.

Paul, who saw Christ in person on the road to Damascus, decided to follow Jesus. This was the time and place of his conversion. *But Paul did not receive the Spirit until three days later.*[10]

Although a Christian during those three days of blindness, Paul possessed no ability to do anything exceptional for God. He needed another dimension.

Enter now, Ananias, "a certain disciple at Damascus."[11]

God, who could have filled Paul with the Spirit without involving another person, chose Ananias to share Paul's experience of receiving the Spirit. "And Ananias . . . putting his hands on him said, Brother Saul, the Lord, even Jesus, that appeared unto thee in the way as thou camest, hath sent me, that thou mightest receive thy sight *and be filled with the Holy Ghost.*[12]

Now that Paul had received the Spirit, he, like Jesus, had a mission. "And straightway he preached Christ in the synagogues, that he is the Son of God."[13]

Consider also the Christians at Samaria. Converted by the Christ-centered preaching of Philip, "they believed Philip preaching the things concerning the kingdom of God, and the name of Jesus Christ, they were baptized, both men and woman."[14] At this point they had salvation, but they had not journeyed beyond it. The Bible states this clearly: "Now when the apostles which were at Jerusalem heard that Samaria had received the word of God, they sent unto them Peter and John: who, when they were come down, prayed for them, that they might receive the Holy Ghost: (for as yet he was fallen upon none of them: only they were baptized in the name of Lord Jesus.) Then laid they their hands on them, and they received the Holy Ghost."[15]

So great is the change brought on by receiving the Holy Spirit that when a magician named Simon "saw that through laying on of the apostle's hands the Holy Ghost was given, he offered them money, saying, Give me also this power, that on whomsoever I lay hands, he may receive the Holy Ghost."[16]

Could it be that many lack the filling of the Spirit because they resisted as did the Jews? Or are unaware of it as were the Samaritans? Or fear it, because it might radicalize their lives, make them unpopular, and ultimately get them in trouble, as it did for Stephen?

Or do they reject the laying on of hands? This simple, biblical procedure cannot be considered radical or fanatical. The washing of feet in the communion service and baptism by immersion, entirely under water, could be considered more "radical."

Just as baptism by water is a clear outward sign of the inner spiritual experience of forgiveness and resurrection to a new life, so the laying on of hands is an outward expression of the inner reception of the power to live the new victorious life for God.

Of course one can receive the filling of the Holy Spirit without having someone else lay hands on, just as forgiveness of sin and eternal life can be experienced without being baptized in water, as was the case, for example, with the thief on the cross. However, is it not always best to follow biblical example, as we do in the case of water baptism by immersion?

While the laying on of hands for receiving the Spirit may be a relatively new idea for many Christians, it need not be considered traumatic. In an atmosphere of "Koinonia" (or informal Christian fellowship, especially in small sharing-and-prayer groups), it need not and should never be rigidly structured, organized, promoted, and programmed. "The wind bloweth where it listeth, and thou hearest the sound thereof, but canst not tell whence it cometh, and whither it goeth: so is every one that is born of the Spirit."[17]

On several occasions I have participated or assisted in this beautiful experience. Any Christian who personally feels the assurance both of salvation and the filling of the Spirit may assist. Whether with just one person, or with a husband and wife, or with a group of six to ten, I have always witnessed an informal, open atmosphere without undue or unhealthy emotionalism but with genuine agapē love, closeness, reverence, peace, and joy. Those present have always expressed their certainty that they have received what they asked for.

Since God is a Spirit, the only realistic way to truly grow close and intimate with God is to become Spirit-filled. Whenever the Holy Spirit takes up residence on the inside, a deep, personal fellowship with God always results. Tragically, the experience of the Spirit has come to be associated in many minds with exterior phenomena—hand-clapping and jazzy music at boisterous mass rallies—*whereas calm peace, gentle love, and quiet service are the true evidences.*

Dr. J. Wilbur Chapman is another Christian who became very successful for God only after a personal encounter, at a specific time, with the Holy Spirit. For five years, Dr. Chapman struggled for the greater victory and power he knew he needed in his life and ministry. Like the disciples of Ephesus, he felt a great lack.

The Christians at Ephesus had been converted and baptized, but when Paul found them, "he said unto them, Have ye received the Holy Ghost since ye believed? And they said unto him, We have not so much as heard whether there be any Holy Ghost."[18] Here again is clear biblical evidence of saved Christians who had yet to experience Spirit-filling.

When God showed Chapman his need of a total surrender of everything he had and everything he was, he could say, " I am willing to be made willing about everything." Later, he says, "At last my will was surrendered. . . . Then without emotion, I said, 'My Father, I now claim from thee the infilling of the Holy Spirit.' From that moment to this he has been a living reality." Chapman said that he had never known what it was to love deeply even his own family, had never known what it was to study deeply the Bible, before that time. "And why should I," he asked, "for had I not just then found the key? I never knew what it was to preach before. Old things are passed away in Christian experience. Behold, all things are become new."

Catherine Marshall, whose books (*A Man Called Peter, Beyond Ourselves, Something More, To Live Again, Meeting God at Every Turn,* and others) have brought spiritual blessing and comfort to millions, was not always a successful witness. In 1944 she began to feel the need for something more in her spiritual life. She devoted a minimum of an hour a day that summer to studying with just a concordance and the Bible to find out all she could about the Spirit. What she found thrilled her.

She yearned to receive this baptism. "Since at that time I had no group to lay hands on me, very quickly and undramatically I asked for the gift of the Spirit. The setting was my bedroom with no other human being present. I knew too that when we accept one of heaven's gifts like that—so quietly in the now—we cannot demand instantaneous proof that the Lord has heard and answered. For that would be walking by sight, not faith at all. . . . I knew that although I should not deny their validity, I should guard against demanding a highly emotional or dramatic experience as initial proof of my baptism in the Spirit."

The first day nothing overt happened. "I experienced no waves of liquid love or ecstatic joy," she says. "But then, in the next few days, quietly but surely, the heavenly Guest made known His presence in my heart. . . . Day by day came the evidence that after I had asked the Helper to enter and take charge, He had done exactly that."

The Spirit became very precious and real to Catherine, helping her to overcome such things as speaking carelessly, critically, and sarcastically. She discovered "the manifestation of His presence on which the Spirit places highest value is the power to witness effectively to others of Jesus." "He then entered into my prayer life and began directing that." "He became the major creative Agent in my writing. In the months that followed and indeed, on down the years, He would methodically bring one area of life after another under His control—health, finances, ambition, reputation. I soon realized that the baptism of the Holy Spirit was no onetime experience, rather a process that would continue throughout my lifetime."[19]

So we see the Spirit's power and presence in the Old Testament, a great movement with tongues of fire in the New, and even now in your day and mine, men and women still being strangely and deeply moved.

Helper, Friend, Comforter, Teacher, Empowering Force, Gentle Guide, the very essence of divine compassion—this wonderful, mysterious, marvelous Being, Heaven's great gift, waits for your invitation.

10

Before You Go On

But be ye doers of the word, and not hearers only.
James 1:22.

Reader, I make an unusual request: If you have yet
to claim the filling of the Holy Spirit by faith by the
time you have read to the end of this chapter, please
put this book down.

You see, the Holy Spirit is a topic that can be treated
like no other. You cannot study it without being pro-
foundly affected. Much more is involved than just acquiring theological information. The Holy Spirit is
more than a concept. He is a living, dynamic, powerful
force in today's world. *He is not ignorable.* Those
who know as much about Him as you do now are com-
pelled by His sheer significance to accept or reject
Him.

If at this point you do not have the personal assurance of being filled with the Spirit, then you should do
one of two things: Seek the filling without delay. Or, if
you do not feel ready, put down this book and go to the
Bible and study for yourself.

When Catherine Marshall felt a growing hunger for
the presence of the Spirit, she decided "to go to the
one place I could count on for final authoritative
truth—the Bible. From long experience I know that

the well-worn words from an old church ordinance had it exactly right—the Bible still is 'the only infallible rule of faith and practice.' "

Determined to find the truth about the Spirit without extraneous influence, Catherine went directly to Scripture and studied for herself. Every day for one entire summer she studied deeply for a minimum of one hour. "A Bible, a *Cruden's Concordance*, a loose-leaf notebook, pen, and colored pencils were my only tools."

At the end of her quest, she and her husband, Peter, who had later joined her in her search, "asked for the great gift of the Spirit. Very quietly, by faith, we received Him—with immense richness and blessing added to our lives."[1]

At this point in your life you may need to search the Bible for yourself to discover the truth about the baptism of the Spirit. Or you may already have done that. If so, have you personally sought the filling for yourself without delay or excuse? Have you taken God at His word? Are you ready to move from hearer to doer?

If you feel you must wait until everything is entirely clear, until you have heard one more sermon on the Holy Spirit, or read a few more articles on the subject in your church paper, or until a revival occurs, or until the charismatic movement subsides, you may *never* receive it.

Many think they must wait until they are "good enough" to receive the Spirit. But you do not qualify for the filling of the Spirit because of the extent and quality of your personal goodness.

Others wait for someone to lead them. But each individual Christian must study the Bible and appropriate its teachings for himself. While he may be guided and even instructed by other Christians, in the end he must stand with his own convictions derived from his own study of the Bible and his own genuine spiritual experience.

Still others await a perfect understanding of the doctrine of the baptism of the Holy Spirit. *But you will never be able to completely understand the doctrine.* No one will. If you try, you will surely miss this great gift God offers you right now. The Holy Spirit filling, indwelling, within a human being is a divine mystery. We can indeed be sure that God offers it to all believers and that we may freely claim it by faith. "And I say unto you, Ask, and it shall be given you; seek, and ye shall find; knock, and it shall be opened unto you. . . . If ye then, being evil, know how to give good gifts unto your children; how much more shall your heavenly Father give the Holy Spirit *to them that ask him.*[2]

At this moment the filling of the Spirit is God's growing edge for many believers. For all Christians the acceptance or rejection of this experience will determine more than anything else what kind of contribution they will make in the final, dramatic effort God has initiated to bring an end to evil in the world and set up the kingdom of heaven. This is true because the Spirit empowers for service as nothing else can.

If you have yet to experience this filling, I want to emphasize to you my testimony: You will experience a highly personal intimacy with God attainable in no other way. One can sing Christian songs and still be nonspiritual, can "do theology" without knowing the Lord in heart and soul, can preach without the animation of the Spirit, can read the entire Bible and receive nothing more than from some other moral-ethical book. But when the Holy Spirit comes to touch the life, spiritual things begin to be spiritually discerned. Then when the Spirit enters *in* to the believer after conversion, the greatest possible fellowship and intimacy with God begins.

Spiritual growth, spiritual experience, spiritual satisfaction cannot be obtained through knowledge alone. Theological knowledge is only a tool, a servant for the believer. For many it has become a trap, a counterfeit of genuine spiritual growth and experience. The preaching, the intellectual understanding of even the finest truths is pointless unless it leads into a personal experience with God. Even the Bible cannot be—but can only bear witness of—the center of Christianity. God is the center. As Paul wisely counseled, "For the kingdom of God is not in word, but in power."[3]

The symbol of the ultimate relationship between God and His believers most used in Scripture is marriage. This is appropriate, for no human relationship is as intimate. And at its best such intimacy results from the experience of genuine love, which goes far beyond merely an experience of the intellect. Two books—Ecclesiastes and the Song of Solomon—adjoin one another in the Bible. The first tells us pointedly that one cannot achieve fulfillment through knowledge alone, warning, "For in much wisdom is much grief; and he that increaseth knowledge increaseth sorrow."[4] "All is vanity—without the remembrance of one's Creator.[5] The second, however, in its profound way says that an ultimate, satisfying relationship with God is based on adoring, intimate love. And the Holy Spirit is the source of this love for "the love of God is shed abroad in our hearts by the Holy Spirit which is given unto us."[6]

What Christ offers us in the gift of the Holy Spirit is not only power for service but a special, divine oneness with God in love, a foretaste of life in heaven above. No one needs wait until eternity begins to experience something so freely offered to all believers right now.

You may accept the gift of the Spirit and begin this closeness with your heavenly Father. You may accept the promised power that will make you a dynamic doer, God's ally in the conquest of the world with love and the ultimate defeat of evil. To delay is to reject by default and to become a bench warmer, watching someone else win the game, while hoping to share in the fruits of victory.

Too many Christians sit idly, waiting for a spiritual handout from God. Too many stand in spiritual welfare lines with their hands out who should be sharing what bread of life they already have with a starving world. Too many queue up for spiritual food stamps who could be working productively in the Master's harvest. Too many seek to be continuously taught who should be teaching. Too many sit back listening to sermons who should be preaching. Too many read who should be writing. Christians under the power of the Spirit have yet to achieve their greatest for God. The best books have yet to be written, the greatest sermons have yet to be preached, the finest songs yet to be composed. Too many ask "Why am I not being shown more love?" who should be expressing the love already shown them.

The world today needs great lovers, individuals so filled with the Spirit that every word and deed—the very expressions on their faces—communicate the Spirit within.

Many believers, so preoccupied with their own sins and weaknesses, need to accept the surety of their own salvation—just as God has offered it. They need to grow up spiritually to meet heart-and-soul needs with the power of the Holy Spirit.

You need not worry whether you understand the theology of the Holy Spirit perfectly. You need not worry whether you may be caught up in counterfeit enthusiasm. You do need to ask, "Am I ready to enter into a special, intimate oneness with God? Am I ready to stop being a hearer only and start being a doer? Do I want to be a receiver only or also a giver?" Jesus promised, "He that believeth on me, as the Scripture hath said, out of his belly shall flow rivers of living water. (But this spake he of the Spirit, which they that believe on him should receive.)"[7]

11

Beyond the Baptism
of the Spirit

This I say then, Walk in the Spirit.
Galatians 5:16.

When asked why he referred to receiving many infillings of the Spirit, a grand old Christian preacher, who had brought thousands to Christ, replied, "I leak!"

The concept of "once filled, always filled with the Spirit" is no more biblically sound than "once saved, always saved." The Bible would have us continually being filled, continually being baptized. The intial baptism of the Spirit is not a once-and-once-only affair, not an instant cure for a bad temper or some other sin problem. It is a starting point, a launching pad, the beginning of a new life of dependence on the indwelling Saviour—a habitual, daily infilling.

Because of sinful human nature which you and I will possess until the return of Christ, our spiritual life tends always toward its own level if separated from the indwelling presence of God. The baptism of the Spirit is your ticket to the Spirit-filled life, that marvelous journey toward the kingdom which progresses as you choose closeness with and control from the Spirit every day. It entitles you to begin the great adventure that makes every hour of your life the finest.

God prizes your human individuality too much to have you lose it even in something as good as the indwelling of the Spirit. In His wisdom, God makes the Spirit-filled life available to you on a daily, voluntary basis in order to preserve your personal freedom, to complement your selfhood. It thus becomes most meaningful and beautiful as manifest in your own personality and character.

As all freedoms do, however, this very freedom, precious as it is, presents a danger. Unless you consciously choose to pursue the Spirit-filled life, it will elude you. Here are guidelines for retaining the Spirit-filled life of the newly Spirit-baptized Christian.

Guideline one: *The experience must be renewed daily if you wish to continue to have it.* How you do this is your choice. But some time and some way each day, you must put your selfhood continuously into the hands of God.

Guideline two: *Never think you are better than one who has yet to chose this baptism.* Remember, your life in the Spirit as always a gift from God. You did not receive it because of your own goodness; you have it only because of the graciousness of God.

God has deposited the wealth of the Spirit in each Christian's bank account. The only difference a Christian who has received this baptism and a brother who has not is that you draw on this treasure.

The only way the filling of the Spirit will make you "greater" is in greater service to others. Compared to Webster's the Bible's definition of greatness is shockingly different: "Among you, whoever wants to be great must be your servant, and whoever wants to be first must be the willing slave of all."[1]

Remember, Christianity is largely one beggar telling another beggar where the bread is. The fact that you may have found more spiritual food than someone else does not mean that you are no longer a beggar! You are just a beggar with more to share!

Guideline three: *Do not expect an immediate sign that you are Spirit-filled.* The baptism of the Spirit is a new adventure in and a new dimension of faith. If a sign always accompanied its reception, it would cease to be a matter of faith. "We receive the promise of the Spirit." says the Scripture, "through faith."[2]

If speaking in tongues or feeling electric or seeing the New Jerusalem in vision or experiencing some other miraculous manifestation always accompanied receiving the Spirit, then the value of faith would be diminished. The outward phenomena would become the proof.

God has said that He wants to give the Spirit to His children even more than we want to give gifts to our own. God also says that if we ask *anything* according to His will it will be given to us. Since God is not a liar, when in faith you request the Spirit, you will receive Him. Your request and your trust allow God to provide the reality to you. These two factors are all the assurance you need. To those who still feel they need a sign to confirm a spiritual experience, Jesus says, "Blessed are they that have not seen, and yet have believed."[3]

Guideline four: *The filling of the Spirit is not determined by your feelings.* Your assurance of Spirit-filling is no more related to the ups and downs of your human emotions than is your assurance of salvation. At times after you have received the baptism you will not always *feel* Spirit-filled. On the contrary, you may even feel bereft. You will still make mistakes, you will still experience discouragement, you will still feel anger, and you will still fall victim to depression. But this does not mean you are not Spirit-filled.

How you handle your hostility and how you let your

other emotions affect yourself and others *will begin to change* after you have received the Spirit. But you will still be a growing Christian, learning from your mistakes until Christ comes. The baptism of the Spirit is no quick-and-easy cure-all for personality defects or character faults. It results in a long-term prescription that must be followed the rest of your life. It is given to empower you for service, not to perfect you instantly. Satan will strive to convince you that you are not Spirit-filled. He will mock you within your own mind. "Look at you!" he will scoff. "You're no different from the way you were before! Here you are, claiming to be Spirit-filled—but, my! how impulsively you reacted to your husband last night! How angry you got with your own child this morning! Now tell me you claim to be Spirit-filled! Why pretend to be something you aren't?" Why will Satan attack so viciously? Because he fears a single Spirit-filled Christian more than an army of unfallen angels!

If you rely on feelings to verify your experience with the Spirit every day, you will weaken and eventually be defeated. You must continually realize that your relationship with the Spirit is based on the set of your will—the vital, daily, conscious choice to have Him continue to live within you.

As a Spirit-filled believer, no longer under bondage to your feelings or even your failings, you claim victory over a bad temper or any other bad habit, even over a lack of love. In the teeth of the devil's attempts to convince you otherwise, you will at last have the power to overcome such things. If you find yourself slipping, do not dwell on your faults. Do not let your sins pull you down. If your temper, for example, has flared, say, "Wait a minute! Part of my promised heritage as a Spirit-filled Christian is to have Jesus' spirit of gentleness and patience in me. *I claim that now as my spiritual right!*"

Guideline five: *You do not have to be able to completely explain or even understand the baptism of the Spirit in order to receive it.* The Holy Spirit is mysterious, and His works in many ways are a deep mystery which human minds cannot fully comprehend.

I know very little about the complicated hydraulic control system of a Boeing 747 jetliner. This does not keep me from riding in one. Even the pilots who fly this giant aircraft do not fully understand this system. But does this fact stop them from flying this plane? If you feel you have to know every detail about the filling of the Holy Spirit before it can become a reality in your life, you will never get off the ground.

The Bible makes no attempt to explain the working of the Spirit fully. For one thing it does not limit Him to certain patterns of operation. Thus never try to force your concept or your experience with the Spirit on another. Jesus compared the Spirit and Spirit-born person to the wind. "The wind bloweth where it listeth, and thou hearest the sound thereof, but canst not tell whence it cometh, and whither it goeth: so is every one that is born of the Spirit."[4] Let *Him* work!

A divinely appointed spontaneity comes to the person who chooses the Spirit. Jesus possessed it. He had different priorities from those of others. Priorities others often failed to understand. Once He began His ministry He followed no rigid routine. *His first priority was to maintain His closeness to His Father and His daily indwelling by the Spirit.* The rest He left confidently to God. In fact, so emptied was He of self that He made no plans of His own! With unruffled calm He accepted God's plans and God's leading one day at a time.

Often the Spirit used the circumstances and people around Christ to direct Him. You and I can allow the Spirit to lead us like that. He can uncomplicate and unstructure our frantic lives, then shape them into a simple outworking of His will. Jesus did this perfectly.

Guideline six: *Sooner or later the experience will get you into trouble*. Long ago Paul said, "All that will live godly in Christ Jesus shall suffer persecution."[5] Little persecution exists today—sad evidence that few are truly Spirit-filled. Since the experience instantly makes you a member of a minority, maybe a minority within a minority, you may find yourself in deep trouble. You will end up separating more and more from the world and its views. You will notice yourself becoming more and more out of step with the world's ideas, the world's goals, the world's entertainment. You will become different, even peculiar. No longer valuing the things many others cherish.

Are nonconformists ever popular? Have they not always made others uncomfortable? In a world of conformists, as someone has wisely put it, anyone heading the opposite direction will appear to be going backward!

Have we forgotten that we Christians are at war? We live in a battle zone, enemy-occupied territory. Of course, such conditions can never be easy. Satan rules—or claims to. As far as the world is concerned, full-fledged citizens of the heavenly kingdom are definitely persona non grata on this planet right now!

"Ye shall be hated of all men for my name's sake," warned Jesus. "Think not that I am come to send peace on the earth: I came not to send peace, but a sword. For I am come to set a man at variance against his father, and the daughter against her mother. . . . A man's foes shall be they of his own household."[6]

Christ was perfect and totally Spirit-filled. He never harmed anyone, devoting all His energy instead to healing and loving. But look at the trouble He got into! After He received the baptism of the Holy Spirit His life became a virtual storm center! People either hated

Him with fervor or loved Him with passion. Some hated Him so much they wanted Him dead, plotted His death, and eventually got their wish.

Since selfishness is the antithesis of love, one cannot tolerate the other. Jesus proved this principle. Nor can falsehood abide truth, nor immorality purity. "For everyone that does evil hateth the light, neither cometh to the light, lest his deeds be reproved."[7]

Being Spirit-filled brings the fullness of Jesus Christ. To have the Spirit *live* in you, to allow Him to possess and control you, to freely admit that you want to do *only* what He asks. What else can make you so extraordinarily different?

By the world's definition, Jesus Christ was radical. Being baptized with the Spirit may radicalize you too, in the sense that it makes you more like Him than anything else. As one writer put it, "Christ had extreme social and economic postures." That is an abstract way of saying He cared nothing for popular opinion or worldly power. After starting His ministry under the direction of the Holy Spirit, He held no regular job. Society considered Him a drifter, moving often from place to place with nowhere to sleep or to call home. He opened no "bank account": lived in poverty on the charity of others.

Jesus heard voices, saw things others couldn't, loved those who hated Him and wanted Him dead, taught strange things about "dying in order to live" and "giving in order to receive." Is this not very odd? He uttered what one modern psychiatrist has in horror called "the most unfortunate guilt-producing statement ever laid on the human race"—Jesus' observation that "whosoever looketh on a woman to lust after her hath committed adultery with her already in his heart."[8]

Imagine the following reactions your Spirit-filling

might provoke in those Jesus still seeks:

"You what? You sold your TV set! Isn't that rather fanatical? Why, how can you now keep in step with the rest of the world?"

"What do you mean you think sending your children to a parochial school is better for them? You mean the school where I send my kids is not good enough for yours, huh?"

"You aren't going to let that outfit walk all over you like that, are you? Listen! I would sue them so fast they'd stumble all over themselves!"

"A conscientious objector? Draft dodger, you mean! Don't you love your country?"

"You're kidding! You stayed up *all* night reading the Bible and praying? You should take better care of your health."

"You are going to quit your second job to have more time to spend with your kids? I can see right now you'll never get ahead!"

"You mean you actually quit your job just to have more time to study the Bible with people? Why don't you let your preacher do that? Isn't that what you pay him for? Besides, you don't have the training for that anyway."

"What are you trying to do? Make the rest of us feel guilty?"

Rufus Mosely wrote, "The average spiritual temperature in the church is so low that when a healthy man comes along, everyone thinks he has a fever!"

The most radical and most important changes in a Spirit-filled person will not be seen in his outward behavior. The gradual inner changes count most. Among these are the tranquility that replaces tension, the peace that expels fear, the forgiveness that drives away hostility and revenge, the praise in the heart that swallows up dissatisfaction, the contentment with all things the acceptance of all people, the unfailing love, the joy unquenchable.

Guideline seven: *In spite of the importance of your experience with the Holy Spirit, keep always in mind that the cross is still central to your Christian life.*

If he had one sermon to preach, I once asked George Vandeman, nationally known speaker on the "It is Written" television program, what topic would he choose? Secretly pleased at my cleverness in asking such a question, I assumed I would have him on hold for many seconds as he flashed through a thousand ideas. I was wrong. As soon as I had finished the question, a smile instantly lighted his face, and without pausing he said, "Why, of course, *the cross!*"

As important as the baptism of the Holy Spirit is, it must never be allowed to replace the priority of the cross in a Christian's life. The cross alone makes eternal life and the gift of the Spirit a reality.

To emphasize the filling of the Spirit above salvation by grace alone, to let it replace the central significance of Christ's death on the cross is to lose spiritual perspective. Such a shift of priority would in the end lead you to ignore the sinfulness of sin, the sinfulness of human nature. Pursued far enough, it would cause denial of the value and immutability of God's law. This law is so important that Christ chose to die rather than ignore or change it. Spirit-filled Christians will always need the cross.

Wasn't Paul one of the most Spirit-filled men who ever lived? But he said little about it. He *did* say, "God forbid that I should glory, *save in the cross* of our Lord Jesus Christ"![9]

There is something about kneeling at the foot of the cross each day and looking up to a dying Saviour— who would not be there but for *your* sins—that helps you keep the right perspective on all things.

When Jesus' disciples returned to Him elated and aglow after working for a few days under the Spirit's amazing power, He did not praise but rather cautioned them "Behold, I give you power to tread on serpents and scorpions, and over all the power of the enemy: and nothing shall by any means hurt you. Notwithstanding in this rejoice not, that the spirits are subject unto you; but rather rejoice, because your names are written in heaven."[10]

A well-known magazine each month includes an eye-catching, full-page picture left uncaptioned. The readers are invited to think up an appropriate title for the picture and to send it in for a prize. Think up a caption for a picture illustrating the greatest event the world has ever seen—a picture of Jesus Christ hanging on the cross. My choice is—"This is what I mean when I say I love you."

Love is the bottom line—for all spiritual truth. Love is divine. As we talk of it, learn of it, become filled by the Holy Spirit, we enter personally into the very presence, the very character, the very power of God Himself. The world today, caught up in a love of power, awaits a generation to demonstrate convincingly the superiority of the power of love.

Let us, dear friends, allow the Holy Spirit such free expression in us that we can show others that special sort of love. The love of the "soft answer" that "turns away wrath," the love that "covers a multitude of sins," the love that "knows no limit to its endurance, no end to its trust, no fading of its hope."[11]

With the Spirit's power, let us now begin to conduct ourselves with such remarkable love that those looking back from the vistas of eternity future will say of those who stood for God at the end of earth's history, *"This* was their finest hour."

References

Chapter 1

1. Winston Churchill, address to the House of Commons, June 18, 1940.
2. See Luke 21:26.
3. Proverbs 20:27.
4. Romans 12:21.

Chapter 2

1. Luke 12:15.
2. Matthew 6:33; John 6:27; Matthew 6:19.
3. John 7:38.
4. John 14:6.
5. Matthew 12:30.
6. Matthew 4:18, 19.
7. Matthew 4:20.
8. Matthew 19:21, 22.

Chapter 3

1. Genesis 5:24.
2. Hebrews 5:12-14, NEB.
3. Hebrews 6:1-3, NEB. (Emphasis supplied.)
4. John 5:24, NEB.

5. Romans 5:11. (Emphasis supplied.)
6. Revelation 2:7.

Chapter 4

1. Ephesians 4:28.
2. Matthew 12:43-45.
3. 2 Timothy 3:5.
4. *Against the Tide: The Story of Watchman Nee* (Fort Washington, Penn.: Christian Literature Crusade, 1973), pp. 94, 95.
5. 2 Peter 3:11, 12, TEV.
6. Revelation 12:17, NEB.
7. Ephesians 6:11, 12, 16, 17, NEB.

Chapter 5

1. Illustration based in part on an account in *The Spirit of Christ in Human Relationships* (Grand Rapids, Mich.; Zondervan, 1968), pp. 12, 13.
2. Philippians 3:21.
3. Matthew 19:21, 22.
4. Matthew 19:25.
5. Matthew 19:26.
6. Matthew 5:48.

7. Matthew 5:44-48, RSV. (Emphasis supplied.)

8. Galatians 5:23; Romans 5:5.

9. 1 Corinthians 13:1-3, NASB.

10. Romans 5:5. (Emphasis supplied.)

11. Colossians 3:14.

12. Hebrews 6:1.

13. Romans 15:16.

14. Mark 1:5.

15. Revelation 1:5, 6.

16. 1 Corinthians 6:2, 3.

17. Ephesians 2:4-6.

18. Revelation 2:26. (Emphasis supplied.)

19. Psalm 8:5.

20. Luke 20:36.

21. Matthew 3:11.

22. Revelation 3:18.

23. Revelation 3:17.

24. Ephesians 6:17.

25. *Salvation by Faith and Your Will* (Nashville, Tenn.: Southern Publishing Association, 1978), p. 64. (Venden's emphasis.)

26. *Ibid.*, p. 74. (Emphasis supplied.)

27. *Ibid.*, p. 75. (Emphasis supplied.)

28. Acts 1:4, 5.

29. Ephesians 1:12, 13.

30. Romans 8:1.

31. John 5:30.

32. John 14:12, 16, 17.

Chapter 6

1. The quotations in this narrative are from 1 Kings 18.

2. Exodus 40:33-38.

3. 1 Corinthians 6:19.

4. Ephesians 2:22.

5. Proverbs 20:27.

6. See Acts 17:6.

7. Acts 12:8.

8. 2 Timothy 3:5.

Chapter 7

1. See Revelation 3:17.

2. Hebrews 7:25.

3. *The Pursuit of God* (Harrisburg, Penn.: Christians Publications, Inc., 1948), p. 13.

4. See 1 Corinthians 13:2.

5. James 4:2.

6. Galatians 3:14.

7. Matthew 3:11.

8. See James 5:16.

9. 1 Peter 2:4.

10. 2 Corinthians 5:17.

11. 1 Samuel 10:6-9.

Chapter 8

1. 2 Timothy 4:7.

2. Ephesians 5:18.

3. John 20:22.

4. John 3:5. (Emphasis supplied.)

5. *The Helper* (Waco, Tex.: Word Books, 1979), p. 164.

6. John 7:17. (Emphasis supplied.)

7. John 9:25. (Emphasis supplied.)

8. Matthew 25:26, 30.

9. Romans 8:9. (Emphasis supplied.)

10. 2 Corinthians 5:4, 5, Phillips.

11. Ephesians 1:13, 14, RSV.

12. 1 Corinthians 6:11.

13. John 21:3.

14. Luke 24:49.

15. *Sit, Walk, Stand* (Fort Washington, Penn.: Christian Literature Crusade, 1957), pp. 54, 55.

16. Zechariah 4:6.

17. *Extraordinary Living for Ordinary Men* (Grand Rapids, Mich.: Zondervan Books, 1965), p. 125.

Chapter 9

1. *The Life of Dwight L. Moody* (New York: Fleming H. Revell Company, 1900), p. 149.
2. Acts 2:22-33.
3. John 14:12.
4. See Acts 6:36-42; 5:3; 8:39; 3:1-11; 16:16-19.
5. John 5:30.
6. Luke 4:1, 14, 18. (Emphasis supplied.)
7. Acts 4:8.
8. Acts 6:5.
9. Acts 7:51. (Emphasis supplied.)
10. Acts 9:9.
11. Acts 9:10.
12. Acts 9:17. (Emphasis supplied.)
13. Acts 9:20.
14. Acts 8:12.
15. Acts 8:14-17.
16. Acts 8:18, 19.
17. John 3:8.
18. Acts 19:2.
19. *The Helper*, pp. 68-70.

Chapter 10

1. *The Helper*, pp. 11-13.
2. Luke 11:9, 13.
3. 1 Corinthians 4:20.
4. Ecclesiastes 1:18.
5. Ecclesiastes 1:1, 8.
6. Romans 5:5.
7. John 7:38, 39.

Chapter 11

1. Mark 10:43, 44, NEB.
2. Galatians 3:14.
3. John 20:29.
4. John 3:8.
5. 2 Timothy 3:12.
6. Matthew 10:22, 34-36.
7. John 3:20.
8. Matthew 5:28.
9. Galatians 6:14. (Emphasis supplied.)
10. Luke 10:19, 20.
11. Proverbs 15:1, RSV; 1 Peter 4:8, RSV; 1 Corinthians 13:7, Phillips.